EULA MAE'S CAJUN KITCHEN

Eula Mae's

CAJUN KITCHEN

Cooking Through the
Seasons on Avery Island

Eula Mae Doré
and Marcelle Bienvenu

Foreword by Paul McIlhenny

THE HARVARD COMMON PRESS

Boston, Massachusetts

The Harvard Common Press
535 Albany Street
Boston, Massachusetts 02118
www.harvardcommonpress.com

Printed in the United States of America
Printed on acid-free paper

LIBRARY OF CONGRESS CATALOGING-IN-PUBLICATION DATA

Doré, Eula Mae.
    Eula Mae's Cajun kitchen : cooking through the seasons on
Avery Island / Eula Mae Doré and Marcelle Bienvenu ; fore-
word by Paul McIlhenny.
        p. cm.
    ISBN 1-55832-240-X (hc : alk. paper)
        1. Cookery, American—Louisiana style. 2. Cookery,
Cajun. 3. Cookery—Louisiana—Avery Island. I. Title.

TX715.2.L68 D67 2002
641.59763—DC21

                                                    2002017270

Special bulk-order discounts are available on this and other
Harvard Common Press books. Companies and organizations
may purchase books for premiums or resale, or may arrange
a custom edition, by contacting the Marketing Director
at the address above.

Jacket design by Night & Day Design
Book design by Richard Oriolo
*All photographs by Brian Smale with the exception of those
on pages ix, 3, 93, 99, 131, and 157, which are used
with permission of the McIlhenny Company Archives*

10 9 8 7 6 5 4 3 2 1

To my daughter, Susan, who persuaded
me to do this book by telling me that
I must leave my collection of recipes
for her, her husband, Todd, and her
sons, Kip and Tyler, and for all
who follow them
—EULA MAE DORÉ

CONTENTS

FOREWORD

About twenty miles south of Lafayette, Louisiana, in the heart of

what is known as Acadiana (also called "Cajun Country"), rising

between Bayou Petite Anse and the Gulf of Mexico, lies Avery

Island, home to nine generations of

my family, the McIlhenny/Avery clan,

and McIlhenny Company, maker of

Tabasco brand pepper sauce.

Lush with acres of blazing

pepper fields interspersed with

majestic stands of live oak and dense, jungle-like bamboo

groves, alive with legions of springtime snowy white egrets,

numerous alligators, and many other exotic and familiar species,

rich in American history and a site of strategic importance during

the Civil War, Avery Island is a singular and unforgettable place.

In the more than 184 years that my family has lived here, untold numbers of people have visited the Island and taken away memories of its distinctive beauty. But very few indeed have stayed long enough to become an irreplaceable part of our custom and culture and to earn the moniker of a treasure of Avery Island. And of these few, none has made a more lasting impression on the hearts and waistlines of so many of us than Eula Mae Doré.

Eula Mae has lived and cooked on Avery Island all of her adult life. My cousins and I were raised on her classic Cajun fare. She lovingly prepared lunch—*étouffées*, gumbos, and jambalayas—for each and every McIlhenny Company employee for the decades she and her husband presided over the Commissary, now known as the Tabasco Deli. Over the years, her breakfasts—biscuits, grits, *boudin*, *pain perdu*, and *andouille*—have become legendary among the many food writers, chefs, and restaurateurs who have been drawn to the birthplace of Tabasco sauce. To her surprise, but not mine, she has been asked many times to share her Cajun techniques with some of the world's most renowned chefs, including Jacques Pépin, Marion Cunningham, and the late Pierre Franey.

In reading this book, it is important to understand that Eula Mae is a classic Cajun (slang for Acadian) cook, not a professionally trained chef. She has never used written recipes, nor has she ever had any formal culinary training, although one would never guess it from the plates she puts in front of you. She cooks only from memory, using recipes developed over a lifetime of experience in her kitchen.

Eula Mae often refers to Avery Island as her Garden of Eden. Its wild blackberries are used in her Blackberry Dumplings, and she grinds its sassafras leaves into *filé* to thicken her gumbos. And while these specific ingredients may not be growing outside your kitchen window, cookbook author Marcelle Bienvenu has spent many hours cooking with Eula Mae, observing her techniques and transcribing her recipes, and she has compiled them in this book so you can now prepare and enjoy the inimitable Cajun dishes that Eula Mae has spent a lifetime perfecting.

PAUL MCILHENNY
President and CEO, McIlhenny Company
Avery Island, Louisiana

ACKNOWLEDGMENTS

Before all others, I must thank Paul "Mr. Paul" McIlhenny, who came up with the idea of putting this book together. I also wish to thank June Gachassin, my daughter's mother-in-law, who took care of Tyler from time to time in order to allow me to work on the book. And a special thanks to Lisa Grant and Mary Beth Farris, who arranged all my test kitchen sessions. Thanks also to Dave Landry and Mable Touchet and all my co-workers throughout the years at Avery Island. They stood by me through all things. And of course, a big thanks to Pam Hoenig and all the staff at the Harvard Common Press who believed in my book. And finally, to my friend Marcelle Bienvenu, who for three years followed me around the kitchen, taking notes, asking questions, listening to my stories, and finally got the book off the ground, I say *bien merci*.

INTRODUCTION

I first encountered Eula Mae Doré (pronounced doh-ray) at the

Commissary on Avery Island, her domain for years, when I went

there about thirty years ago with a friend to have a sandwich.

And what a sandwich it was! Crusty

French bread from LeJeune's Bakery

in Jeanerette was piled high with

thinly sliced ham and dressed with

fresh cold, shredded lettuce, thinly

sliced tomatoes, and sliced dill

pickles!

Eula Mae was bustling in and out of the small kitchen in the

back of the building, saying hello to customers, and somehow

managing to take care of "business." The Island residents

counted on the Commissary for everything from kerosene and

detergent to canned goods, milk, bread, produce, mops, candy,

meats, and soft drinks.

The walls of the Commissary were lined to the ceiling with shelves and Eula Mae could deftly pull down something from the very top shelf with the use of a pole to which was attached a nail or hook. With this very primitive tool, I saw her give a good nudge to a can that would come tumbling down and be caught neatly in her hand. Nothing could intimidate the affable lady who helped to run the store.

Through the years I came across her at various parties held at Marsh House or at private homes on the Island. Again, she was always busy, cooking in the kitchen, arranging trays, passing hors d'oeuvres, greeting guests, and generally running the show from the wings.

When I had a restaurant in the 1980s in Broussard, a few miles from Avery Island, she and I were interviewed by and cooked for *Southern Living* magazine, and I was impressed with her knowledge and graciousness. Later, I would see her photograph and recipes in *Gourmet* magazine and other publications.

Then, about three years ago, I received a call from Paul McIlhenny, president and CEO of McIlhenny Company, maker of Tabasco sauce since 1868. Paul and I have been friends for years, sharing a great love for good food and good times. He wanted me to come and meet with him and Eula Mae and discuss the possibility of doing a cookbook featuring her recipes. I was delighted.

We gathered in Paul's office on a beautiful bluebird autumn day with nary a cloud in the sky and just a hint of coolness in the air. We chatted and I felt Eula Mae's shyness and reluctance at taking on such a project. Before we parted, I asked if she would just sit and chat with me for a while in the sitting room adjacent to Paul's office.

As we spoke, I studied her features. Her strawberry blond tresses, threaded with a few silver hairs, were softly arranged in a "Gibson Girl" do, and her face was almost as smooth as a teenager's. I noticed too that there was not much makeup, just a touch of pink on her soft lips. Her eyes were the color of good bourbon. She certainly didn't look like a lady of seventy-one years!

She told me of her mother's death at an early age, leaving Eula Mae and her father, Seymar Touchet, to deal with the other children—Euel, twelve years old, Earline, two and a half years old, and Wilfred, about five months old.

"I was so sad, not only because I missed her terribly, but also because my father was without the woman he loved," she told me.

"I had to quit school at age ten to care for the younger children, and try to make a home for my father. That was what inspired me to cook. I wanted to please him and bring a smile to his face! I really had to teach myself. Even at so young an age I knew what dishes tasted like and I had to learn to duplicate that. We didn't have cookbooks and, even if we did, I could barely read."

But, of course, cookbooks were not generally around in Cajun country in the 1930s and 1940s. Most everyone learned by watching and listening to "the old ones," who were masters in the kitchens of south Louisiana. Although Eula Mae didn't have her mother (Estella Doré; yes, another Doré) to guide her in the kitchen, she learned some tricks of the trade from her grandmother Cecile Leonard. Mrs. Leonard lived in nearby St. Martinville on a sugarcane farm, where she raised fourteen of her own children as well as seven orphans.

"Her stove never got cold, I can tell you," remembers Eula Mae. "She was a great baker and it was from her I learned how to make biscuits and bread."

Eula Mae's father was a farmer on land he owned in Coteau, a small community near New Iberia, and not far from the Island. He raised cotton, sugar cane, corn, and peppers. (When her brothers went out on their own, they raised peppers on Jefferson Island for the McIlhenny Company.)

"Daddy never had time to cook. He was in the fields from daybreak to sundown and depended on me to provide all the meals for the family. And we all had chores. We milked the cows, fed the chickens and geese, picked eggs, and prepared the meals that were taken to the farmhands in the fields. Sometimes my grandmother helped me make cornbread, biscuits made with lard, and lots of grits to take to the workers. These items were not costly since we had just about everything on hand on the farm. What we didn't have, we bartered for, like syrup, cornmeal, and stone-ground flour."

Eula Mae and her siblings picked pecans on their land to help pay for clothes, shoes, and a few extras.

Boucheries (hog slaughters) were held two or three times a year during the winter months. Families gathered to slaughter the hogs that then provided pork chops and hams. The trimmings were made into *boudin*, a sausage made with bits of pork, onions, and rice. Some of the leaner trimmings were smoked to make *tasso*, which was used to season stews, vegetables, and jambalayas. The pork skin was made into *gratons*, or cracklings, as they are called locally. Cuts of the hog were also used to make fresh sausage as well as *andouille*, a smoked sausage. The hog's stomach was stuffed with bits of pork mixed with vegetables; called *chaudin*, it was considered a gastronomic treat.

"We used everything from the hog but the squeal," says Eula Mae.

Eula Mae also remembers that all the laundry was done by hand. This was before disposable diapers and all the diapers had to be washed, dried, and folded. Most of the children's clothes were made from flour sacks, which at the time were colorful and ideal for making skirts.

"We made our own starch on the stove. A light starch was used for delicate clothes like the children's shirts and skirts. Heavier starch was used for work clothes for my father. Doing laundry was backbreaking. Clean items were dipped in the starch and wrung. Then they were hung on the clothesline. After they were dry, they were sprinkled with water, then rolled up and wrapped in oil cloth to cure before they were ironed."

After World War II, her father made a bit of money growing cotton.

"I'll never forget Daddy buying me a blue coal oil stove as well as a blue iron that was run by propane gas. Both made my life a lot easier."

In 1947, Eula Mae met her husband-to-be, Walter Doré.

"I met him in a cane field where he was working at the time," she related. "Some friends and I went to pick some sweet cane to peel, cut, and chew. Ah, the pieces of the sweet cane were so good. It was better than candy!"

Walter asked her if the cane was sweet.

"I told him yes, it was," she said.

And two years later, in 1949, they married in New Iberia.

"Our wedding was very simple. I didn't have a white wedding dress and my only attendants were the employees at the rectory. After the simple ceremony, we went back to the farm to work. There was always so much to do."

Being young and newly wed, they didn't have a home or many belongings, so they moved in with Walter's uncle, who worked on Avery Island.

Walter's great aunts and uncles had raised him, because his parents died when he was young, and it was they who gave him the nickname of MoNeg. When they moved to the Island, Eula Mae decided that she would not use the name Walter for him and from then on she called her Walter "MoNeg."

"You see, it was the late Walter S. McIlhenny, then president of McIlhenny Company, who allowed us to come and live on the Island and I decided there should be only one Walter on the Island."

Eula Mae's first job on the Island was working at the factory with the machines that capped the Tabasco sauce bottles.

"I did this from six A.M. to ten A.M., then took a break. In the afternoon, at four o'clock, I reported to the Commissary to Hilda Desormeaux and Leona Rodrigue, who managed the store. I helped to stock the shelves, took inventory, and made orders," she remembered.

The nearest grocery store was several miles away in New Iberia and most of the resident workers on the Island didn't have cars.

"Also, you see, there were a lot of the McIlhenny family living on the Island and they would send in their grocery orders to the Commissary. Then, we had to take their list and gather all the items for them to pick up when the order was completed."

MoNeg's first job on the Island was with the landscaping crew. At the time, land was being cleared along the marsh that bordered the pepper fields. "MoNeg wasn't very well educated, but he surely knew how to work. He operated large tractors and dirt movers, and believe it or not, some of that work still stands today," Eula Mae told me proudly.

In 1953, she and MoNeg were able to move into a home of their own in the area on the Island called "the Tango," where workers lived in small cottages lined up in neat rows, with space for home gardens.

"I was so pleased to have our own home," said Eula Mae, "and I thanked Mr. Walter for that."

It was during this time that the butcher at the Commissary wanted to retire and Mr. Walter asked MoNeg to train for the job. Not long after, the two ladies who managed the Commissary also retired and Mr. Walter offered the job of running the store to MoNeg and Eula Mae.

"Oh, my, we were so pleased to run the Commissary, since it was like having our own business. MoNeg would open up the store at four A.M. and make coffee for the workers on the Island. I came in at five-thirty and began getting things ready for the day."

Soon they had a bustling business going. Eula Mae came up with the idea of selling sandwiches at lunchtime. Her famed sandwiches and po-boys became legend, so much so that businessmen from New Iberia, about eight miles away, drove to the Island for lunch.

Eula Mae offered sandwiches on white Evangeline Maid bread or on LeJeune's French bread, which came fresh from the ovens in nearby Jeanerette.

"Let's see, we had ham, cheese, roast beef, baloney, and you could have any combination of those. Then we had what I called 'load the wagon' po-boys, which had a little of everything on it. I carefully spread the bread with mayonnaise, then sprinkled Tabasco sauce on it and spread it evenly with a knife. That was the secret to those good sandwiches!" said Eula Mae with a laugh.

It wasn't long before MoNeg came up with the idea of bringing lunch to the workers in the field.

"Oh, yes, MoNeg was very innovative, and he also loved life, and enjoyed preparing food for everyone, including Mr. Walter and his friends. He fashioned a truck on which he could carry everything for making sandwiches, as well as lemonade and ice. He took this truck to the pepper fields so the workers could have something to eat and drink when they took a break from picking peppers. My job every morning was to help him cut all the meats and cheese, pack the bread, and make lemonade," recalled Eula Mae fondly.

Soon MoNeg was able to convince Mr. Walter to allow him to add on a bigger kitchen at the rear of the Commissary. There he had a huge meat slicer, a large mixer, and a stove on which he could prepare anything from gumbo to jambalaya for McIlhenny parties or special occasions.

"And I convinced Mr. Walter to let me have a cottage behind the restaurant where I could also have a small fenced-in garden," she explained. "Mr. Walter was something else! He asked

MoNeg and me to show him exactly where we wanted it. And he had our old cottage moved from the Tango to the spot we had chosen, under some old oak trees. Now, tell me if Mr. Walter wasn't generous and understanding? I appreciated all that he did for us."

In 1960, MoNeg and Eula Mae had a daughter, Susan, who is their only child. There are two grandsons, Kip, who is now twenty-three, and Tyler, ten.

Her soft eyes watered as she told me about MoNeg passing away suddenly in 1982. It was a great personal loss as well as a loss to the residents on the Island.

"But I knew I had to continue running the Commissary. It was my job and I loved it," she said.

It was her life, she explained. She so enjoyed keeping busy, serving her customers, and having children come in and out of the store.

Barbara and Rosemary McIlhenny, daughters of Paul McIlhenny, often came to the Commissary, when they were young children, for "mushy" ham sandwiches. Even when Eula Mae cut up everything for their mother to make the sandwiches, the girls would say, "Mom, you don't make them like her."

"I told them the one missing ingredient was my special TLC—tender, loving care."

And it's with that special TLC that Eula Mae prepares everything! Nothing is ever too hard or time-consuming for Eula Mae to do. Watching her do something as simple as chopping onions or vegetables is like observing an act of reverence.

"*Chère*, everything you do, do it with love and happiness. What you give will return to you many times over, *oui*!" I remember her telling me.

She often adds a word or two of French in our conversations because that was the language she spoke as a young girl.

"And you know, darling, French phrases and comments that we use in south Louisiana often say it better, *non*?" she said with a smile.

Eula Mae continued to run the Commissary on her own until 1991.

We finished our chat and I went on my way, excited by the possibility of working on the cookbook project.

Several days later, I learned that Eula Mae felt she wouldn't have time to work with me. I was disappointed. But somehow Paul and his cousin Took Osborn were able to convince her to reconsider. She did, and not but two months later we began testing her recipes.

We went to work at the kitchen at the McIlhenny Company complex. It is a familiar place for Eula Mae, since she often prepares meals there for visitors and business people who come to the Island. Paul offered to buy her any pots and pans she wanted for the testing, but she graciously refused, saying that her old pots and pans would work just fine. I realized that she had been cooking in the same pots for thirty or more years and is more comfortable with them. In addition, I learned while we were cooking that she knew the measurements for her collection of cookware.

The first day we met, I arrived with my laptop, measuring spoons and cups, a small kitchen scale, and a tape measure.

Noticing her shyness, I assured her that I was not a trained chef, only a food writer. I reminded her that she had cooked alongside the late Pierre Franey, Jacques Pépin, Marion Cunningham, and Sheila Lukins, even showing them a trick or two in the kitchen, and I was certainly not in that class of gifted people!

When I whipped out my measuring utensils, she quietly told me she had never used any of those before and didn't want to start now. Her measures were done in an old jar, in the palm of her hand, or just by touch and taste.

"Eula Mae," I explained, "You know how much, but people elsewhere need to have measurements."

That settled, we pushed on. By the end of the day, I realized what a special lady and cook she was. I noted that she never wastes anything. The seeds of bell peppers were put in a small container to take home to plant in her garden. The skins from the yellow onions were stowed in a bag.

"Darling, keep the skins and put them in the freezer. Put them in the pot when you're making shrimp stock to make it golden colored."

She uses only fresh garlic.

"Don't buy that garlic in those jars at the supermarket. Peel them yourself. The aroma is wonderful and, of course, the taste is so much better because they're fresh."

And, speaking of garlic, she showed me another trick.

"When cooking dishes like gumbo, stew, jambalaya, or smothered vegetables, I prefer not to add chopped or minced garlic because sometimes the taste is too strong, as far as I'm concerned. I usually put the whole garlic clove, or two or three, in the pot, and let it cook until it melts, or becomes very soft. The garlic flavor is milder, almost sweet. If it doesn't melt or soften, give it a little push against the side of the pot with the back of a spoon. Try it, you'll see!"

Each time we worked, I picked up all kinds of tips.

"I usually use peanut oil, but then again, sometimes vegetable oil or corn oil works better in certain recipes."

"Don't rush when you're making a roux; cook it long and slow. Make the roux a shade darker than you want in the final dish because once you add the onions, bell peppers, celery, and garlic, the roux pales a bit."

"When combining flour and wet ingredients when baking, always stir in one direction. It prevents the mixture from getting tough."

"Always wear a smile. Don't be gloomy. Think of what you can do to make someone's day a little better. Use a little TLC when you're cooking. People do appreciate your efforts."

"It's best to make candy on a cold, dry day."

"When boiling, to keep the pot from overflowing, put a spoon into it. When I see steam rising from the lid of the rice pot, I know to lower the heat."

"When cooking green vegetables like beans or peas, put a leaf of lettuce in the pot to prevent discoloring. When cooking vegetables like cabbage, turnips, and mustard greens, do not overpower them with too much seasoning. They each have their own unique taste and you don't want to ruin that."

"To care for black cast-iron pots, rub them with tallow, the fat from steaks, then put them in the oven or over a high fire and the fat will burn off, making the pots shiny and smooth like satin."

One day, we took a break from our work and drove around the Island, going to areas that are not open to the public. We went to the highest spot on the Island, where she often walks.

"See, darling, how beautiful and lush the Island is! Can you understand why I love this place so?"

We rode past family homes of the McIlhennys and Averys that bore names like Deep Roots, Buzzard's Roost, Sundown, and Deer Run, nestled in the verdant, private wooded areas of the Island. We swung by the swimming pond called the Blue Hole where, during the summer, the McIlhennys and Averys and their guests bask in the sun and enjoy the gentle breezes from nearby Vermilion Bay.

We slowly made our way through the swamp known as the Saline Woods, where we looked for the great blue herons, snowy egrets, and ibises that migrate to the Island at various times of the year. The cacophony emanating from the swamp can be almost deafening. Duckweed forms a bright green carpet on the still water where alligators thrive.

She pointed out the graceful live oak trees from which hung clumps of Spanish moss, what she called "the lace of the Island." We marveled at the wild magnolia trees, and the sweet honeysuckle vines that tangle around fences and barns.

We drove past the pepper fields, the community vegetable garden, and the huge plant where Tabasco sauce is made.

"Ah, can you smell the peppers, *chère*? It's the perfume of the Island!"

I learned about her love and devotion to all of the families of the Island. Many of the children she has helped raise call her Granny. She told me that she adored having youngsters come in the Commissary or stop at her home for a homemade doughnut or a blackberry tart.

And it's nothing to have the McIlhennys call her to prepare a special dish or even to cook everything for a cocktail party or breakfast.

"Since my retirement from the Commissary, I have a new job—cooking for parties, dinners, lunches, and whatever else comes along," she said. "I've known five generations and they are all like my own."

They, in turn, love to show her off. Food writers and television crews are often on the Island to interview and film Eula Mae cooking one of her specialties. One day while I was there, she had to take a break from our testing to tape a show for the PBS series *The Victory Garden*. Another time, she and I were filmed making her delicious crab and shrimp sauce piquante for a Food Network show. Not only can she cook, she also has a personality that is delightful on camera!

I can attest to the fact that she is an energetic nurturer. She has that wonderful sense of *joie de vivre* and is truly a treasure of Avery Island. Her cooking style is simple because that is the approach of true Cajun cuisine. She believes in cooking what is at hand—fresh blackberries, pears, figs, and vegetables—all available on the Island.

"Cook with what you have. As long as it's fresh and prepared with care, your meal will always be delicious!"

She cooks with her heart and soul, and I'm very fortunate to be able to share with you all that she has taught me. The recipes are simple, but classic and traditional to south Louisiana. The dishes are not sophisticated, but you'll find nothing more delicious and delightful. These are dishes that are not commonly found in most restaurants. I like to think of them as things "your mama cooks for you."

So, enjoy, *mes amis*, and *merci beaucoup*, Eula Mae!

SPRING

"When I was a young girl living on my father's farm, spring was
a busy time. Being farmers, we knew how to watch for signs,
like a new moon, or new leaves on pecan trees and, yes, even
the temperature of the soil before we

planted our spring and summer

gardens. Oh, sometimes we had late

frost and lost a few plants, but

usually we were very successful with

our garden. We planted tomatoes,

okra, butter beans, bell peppers, eggplant, yellow squash, and

crowder peas. We also had a big field of corn because we had to

feed our livestock with it."

Since they had no electricity when Eula Mae was growing

up, all the vegetables were "put up" in canning jars.

"There was a room off the kitchen that was used as a pantry. Huge crocks were filled with sausages and other meats preserved in lard. Shelves were stocked with the home-canned goods. We may not have had a lot of money, but we never went hungry."

Eula Mae also remembers her daddy ordering a hundred baby chickens that would eventually grow into spring chickens with plump, wide breasts.

"The postman brought the tiny baby chicks in a big box. They were so little! We were so excited and we were trained to take care of them. We knew, even as children, to keep a lantern lit in their pen to keep them warm. I remember we had a large jug filled with water and fitted with a rubber cap that had to be hung upside down low enough for the chicks to 'suck' for water. Oh, it was hard work, but we were so careful not to lose any of the chicks because Daddy would have our hide!"

Having lived on Avery Island for more than fifty years, Eula Mae thinks of it as her very own Garden of Eden and particularly so in the spring. After the cold and dismal months of winter, Eula Mae likes to walk around the Island, searching for new growth.

One cool early April morning, I walked with her on the grounds of the Island as she pointed out the new, yellow-green leaves peeking out on the bald cypress trees, and tiny sprouts on the willow trees. Along the fences, she checked the blossoms on the wild black-berry vines that tangled around a wooden fence.

"Once the berries come out, they will be perfect for cobblers, pies, and dumplings," she told me.

She pointed out the sassafras trees that grow wild on the Island.

"*Chère*, long ago the Choctaw Indians that lived in this area of south Louisiana showed the early settlers how to season their food with the ground dried leaves of the sassafras tree. We call it *filé* [fee-lay] powder and use it to thicken our gumbos. It must never be added to the gumbo until the pot is removed from the heat because it will make the gumbo gummy. And, my darling, never use *filé* in a gumbo made with okra. You will have a very stringy or ropey mess!"

We strolled through the area called the Tango, where cottages stand side by side in rows. The residents of the Tango were putting in their summer gardens, which will include tomatoes, eggplant, bell peppers, and perhaps some beans.

"*Chère*, here on the Island we have just about everything we need to make so many good dishes."

As we made our way to Jungle Gardens, planted generations ago by E. A. McIlhenny, the son of the inventor of Tabasco sauce, we spotted several deer that were tame enough to pet.

We saw peacocks perched in an old live oak tree, rabbits hopping through dense foliage, and a few alligators sunning on the banks of a large pond.

I heard the beat of wings and looked up to see a flock of white egrets overhead. Eula Mae told me that in the spring the egrets come home to nest and care for their young in what is called Bird City, located on the edges of the public gardens. And therein lies another story of the Island.

During the late nineteenth century, the gorgeous plumes from the egrets were used to adorn women's fashionable hats and the egrets almost became extinct. But Mr. McIlhenny was able to raise eight of the birds he found in the wild to maturity on the Island. The birds flourished and now thousands come home to nest each spring.

Eula Mae and I paused to watch the snowy white, graceful egrets coming to their nests on raised wooden fixtures over the verdant pond.

"It's magical, don't you think?" Eula Mae whispered to me.

A breeze from nearby Vermilion Bay carried a whiff of salt and water.

"The fresh air that blows from the bay never fails to stimulate me."

She laughed, "Like a child, I can't wait for Easter to come. And *chère*, you haven't seen anything as pretty as when the Island is in full bloom with pink, white, purple, and peach-colored azaleas, white, dainty bridal wreath, Louisiana irises, and scented jasmine vines!"

Thunder announced an approaching storm.

"*Allons!* Let's go make something pretty and good to celebrate this wonderful season of rebirth!" she laughed as we made a run for her neat, cozy house.

MR. WALTER'S DINNER PARTIES

Sausage and Shrimp Gumbo

McIlhenny Chili for the Marines

Smothered Turnips with Pork

Corn Sticks

Smothered Mustard Greens

Mr. Walter's Chocolate Fudge Cake

The late McIlhenny Company president, Walter S. McIlhenny, was an avid hunter and fisherman and also a gracious host. He loved entertaining friends, as well as visitors to the Island.

Mr. Walter's home, cypress-shingled with white pillars and green shutters, was an ideal place for having parties. A large butcher's block measuring six by nine feet stood in the center of his large kitchen. Pots and pans were hung from a rack over the table and a large stove occupied one wall. An autographed photograph of the late James Beard, the renowned chef and food writer, and a frequent visitor to Avery Island, was hung on another wall.

Although his dining room was large, he chose a table that sat no more than eight so that each guest could take part in the dinner conversation.

Mr. Walter was a Marine (he was awarded the Navy Cross and the Silver Star for gallantry on Guadalcanal) and his military buddies often traveled to Avery Island, enjoying many meals at the house or on the grounds.

Mr. Walter dearly loved the Island and went into the fields during pepper picking season to personally weigh the day's picked peppers. He was always attired in a coat and tie, no matter what the temperature!

Willie "Chief" Robertson, Mr. Walter's houseman, often greeted guests at the door, then escorted them in to the large entrance hall, where they were offered cocktails. The hall was filled with prized trophies of his safaris in Africa. Mr. Walter, an accomplished hunter, hunted with the same guide used by Ernest Hemingway and, like Mr. Hemingway, was a great raconteur.

"And he also had a great passion for good food. He enjoyed dining in New Orleans, but he was also just as happy enjoying parties held at his home. He had his own cook, but he often asked my husband, MoNeg, and I to prepare local traditional dishes for his guests, some of whom had never tasted the cuisine of the area. He was known as a gentleman in the truest sense and, when he died in June 1985, I felt a great loss, as did everyone who knew him. I called him Lord of the Island."

"He enjoyed dining in New Orleans, but he was also just as happy enjoying parties held at his home."

Gumbo is usually served as a main course because it is so hearty and filling. But when Mr. Walter had dinner parties, he often served it as a first course.

"He would call me," recalls Eula Mae, "and ask me to prepare a gumbo for him. I can hear him even now. 'What kind do you think would be best, Eula Mae? Whatever you think,' he would say. But I knew he adored sausage and shrimp gumbo."

SAUSAGE AND SHRIMP GUMBO

MAKES 8 SERVINGS

2 tablespoons vegetable oil

1 pound andouille (or other spicy smoked sausage), cut crosswise into $1/4$-inch-thick slices

2 tablespoons all-purpose flour

$1/2$ cup chopped yellow onions

$1/2$ cup seeded and chopped green bell peppers

1 garlic clove, minced

2 cups chicken broth

2 cups sliced fresh okra or one 10-ounce package frozen sliced okra, thawed

$1/2$ teaspoon salt, or more to taste

$1/8$ teaspoon cayenne, or more to taste

$1/2$ teaspoon Tabasco brand pepper sauce

2 bay leaves

1 pound medium-size shrimp, peeled and deveined

$1/4$ cup chopped green onions (green part only)

Hot cooked long-grain white rice (see page 171)

1. Heat 1 tablespoon of the oil in a large skillet over medium-high heat. Add the sausage and cook, stirring frequently, for 5 minutes. Remove the sausage with a slotted spoon and set aside.

2. Heat the remaining 1 tablespoon oil in the same skillet over medium-high heat. Stir in the flour and cook, stirring constantly, until the roux is light brown, about 2 minutes (see page 94 for Eula Mae's advice on making a roux). Add the onions, bell peppers, and garlic, and cook, stirring frequently, until soft, about 5 minutes. Gradually stir in the broth and blend

until smooth. Bring to a boil. Add the sausage, okra, salt, cayenne, Tabasco, and bay leaves, cover, reduce the heat to medium-low, and simmer for 20 minutes.

3. Stir in the shrimp and green onions and simmer until the shrimp turn pink, about 5 minutes. Remove the bay leaves and serve in soup bowls over rice.

When Mr. Walter's Marine buddies would come to the Island, he often hosted casual parties dressed in faded khakis and tennis shoes. He was the ultimate host, always making sure his guests were comfortable and, of course, well fed. He loved to serve his pals this chili because he thought it was just the thing to serve while they reminisced about the old days.

"Sometimes my husband made this chili for Mr. Walter. I always found it strange that he liked it served with rice, but I never questioned it. We are in rice country and if it made Mr. Walter happy, that was fine with me!"

MCILHENNY CHILI FOR THE MARINES

MAKES ABOUT 6 SERVINGS

1/4 cup vegetable oil

3 pounds lean beef chuck, cut into 1-inch cubes

1 cup chopped yellow onions

3 garlic cloves, minced

3 tablespoons chili powder

2 teaspoons ground cumin

2 teaspoons salt

2 teaspoons Tabasco brand pepper sauce

3 cups water

One 4-ounce can chopped green chiles, drained

Hot cooked long-grain rice (see page 171)

Chopped onions for garnish

Shredded Cheddar cheese for garnish

Sour cream for garnish

1. Heat the oil in a large, heavy pot or Dutch oven over medium-high heat. Add the beef and cook, stirring often, until browned well. Transfer the beef to a platter and set aside.

2. Add the onions and garlic to the pot and cook, stirring often, until soft, about 5 minutes. Add the chili powder, cumin, salt, and Tabasco and cook for 1 minute. Add the water and chiles and bring to a boil. Return the beef to the pot and reduce the heat to medium-low. Cover and simmer until the beef is very tender, about 1½ hours.

3. Serve hot over rice and garnish with onions, cheese, and sour cream.

At times, Mr. McIlhenny's parties were grand affairs, but on other occasions, he offered "down-home" food, using vegetables that were grown on the Island.

"He used to tell me that nothing is better than fresh vegetables prepared simply. Whenever possible, *chère*, I picked the turnips the same day I prepared them. Now, what could be fresher?"

This is a dish Eula Mae prepared often for supper for her family, and although it was nothing fancy, everyone, even Mr. Walter, loved it. Serve this hot with Corn Sticks (page 10).

SMOTHERED TURNIPS WITH PORK

MAKES 4 SERVINGS

$1^{1}/_{2}$ pounds fresh pork loin, cut crosswise into $^{1}/_{2}$-inch-thick slices

1 teaspoon salt

$^{1}/_{4}$ teaspoon Accent seasoning

$^{1}/_{4}$ teaspoon cayenne

$^{1}/_{4}$ teaspoon black pepper

$^{1}/_{4}$ cup vegetable oil

8 medium-size turnips (about 2 pounds), peeled and diced

1 cup chopped yellow onions

1 tablespoon sugar

$^{1}/_{3}$ cup chopped green onions (green and white parts)

$^{1}/_{4}$ cup chopped fresh parsley leaves

1. Season the pork slices with the salt, Accent, cayenne, and black pepper.

2. Heat the vegetable oil in a large, heavy pot over medium heat. Add the pork and cook, covered, turning the meat once or twice to brown evenly, about 20 minutes, scraping the bottom and sides to dislodge the browned bits.

3. Add the turnips and onions. Stir to mix, cover the pot, and reduce the heat to medium-low. Cook, stirring occasionally, for 30 minutes, then sprinkle with the sugar. Add the green onions and parsley, cover, and cook for 30 minutes longer, stirring often. The turnips should be soft and mushy and the pork very tender.

The day Eula Mae and I made these corn sticks, I saw that she had brought some old black cast-iron pans in which to cook them. The pans were velvety smooth and I could tell she had cared for them with that TLC of hers throughout the years.

She told me, "I've had these pans for years and carry them with me whenever I go to Marsh House to prepare a breakfast or brunch. The corn sticks are nicer for parties than regular cornbread, don't you think?"

CORN STICKS

MAKES 14 CORN STICKS

3 tablespoons butter, at room temperature, plus $^1/_2$ cup (1 stick) butter, melted

1 large egg

$^1/_4$ cup vegetable oil

1 cup milk, plus $^1/_2$ cup warm milk

1 cup cake flour

$^3/_4$ cup stone-ground yellow cornmeal

2 teaspoons baking powder

$^1/_4$ teaspoon baking soda

1 teaspoon salt

2 tablespoons sugar

1. Grease 2 corn stick pans with the room-temperature butter. Preheat the oven to 400°F. Put the pans in the oven to heat.

2. In a large mixing bowl, whisk together the egg, melted butter, vegetable oil, 1 cup milk, cake flour, and cornmeal. Combine the baking powder, baking soda, salt, sugar, and $^1/_2$ cup warm milk in a small mixing bowl. Pour the milk mixture into the egg mixture and mix well, then pour the batter evenly into the hot corn stick pans.

3. Bake until golden brown, about 20 minutes. Remove from the oven and let cool for a couple of minutes, then turn them out. Serve warm.

South Louisiana cooks like to smother some vegetables to get all the flavors out of them. Eula Mae cooks her mustard greens with salt meat, sometimes called salt pork, to really get lots of flavor.

"Pickled pork has saltpeter and pickling seasoning. Salt meat, on the other hand, is only processed with salt. Now sometimes, salt meat, or salt pork, has a lot of salt and that's why I like to boil it a bit to remove some of that salt. Then again, sometimes it's not real salty!"

Mustard greens, much like collard greens, have a pungent flavor and are grown in home gardens during the winter months in south Louisiana. The leaves are a rich, dark green and grow close to the ground.

SMOTHERED MUSTARD GREENS

MAKES 4 SERVINGS

$3/4$ pound salt meat or salt pork, trimmed and cut into 1-inch cubes

3 quarts water

3 pounds fresh mustard greens, stems removed and rinsed several times in cool water

$1/2$ cup vegetable oil

3 tablespoons all-purpose flour

1 cup yellow onions

1 large garlic clove, peeled

1 teaspoon salt

$1/4$ teaspoon black pepper

$1/4$ teaspoon cayenne

1. Boil the salt meat in enough water to cover in a small saucepan for 30 minutes, then drain and set aside.

2. In a large kettle, put the water to boil over medium-high heat. When it just comes to a boil, add about one third of the greens and, using a large kitchen spoon, press them down. They will wilt. Then add another third and press down, then finally add the remaining greens, firmly press down, and cook until all are wilted. Remove from the heat and drain well in a colander, pressing out any excess water. Pat dry with paper towels, then coarsely chop.

3. Heat the oil for 2 minutes in a large, heavy pot over medium heat. Add the flour and stir constantly until it reaches the color of sandpaper, 3 to 4 minutes. Add the onions, garlic, and salt meat and cook, stirring, for 3 minutes. Add the mustard greens, cover, and cook, stirring occasionally, for 30 minutes. Add the salt, black pepper, and cayenne, stir to mix, and continue to cook until the garlic "melts," or softens, about 15 minutes. Serve hot.

"**M**r. Walter was a chocolate lover. He adored my Chocolate Bread Pudding (page 149), but he also loved this cake. I remember one dinner party when the table was laid with a white linen tablecloth and in the center was a bowl of white camellias from the garden. The men wore black bow ties and white shirts. It was so lovely with the candlelight," remembers Eula Mae.

This cake is sinfully rich. Serve it with a *demitasse* of dark roasted coffee.

MR. WALTER'S CHOCOLATE FUDGE CAKE

MAKES ONE 3-LAYER 8-INCH CAKE; SERVES 8 TO 10

$^1/_2$ cup (1 stick) plus 3 tablespoons butter, at room temperature

2$^1/_2$ cups cake flour

2 cups sugar

$^1/_2$ cup unsweetened cocoa powder

$^1/_2$ cup butter-flavored Crisco vegetable shortening, at room temperature

3 large eggs

1 teaspoon pure vanilla extract

$^1/_2$ cup buttermilk combined with 1 teaspoon baking soda

1 cup milk

Chocolate Pecan Cake Filling (page 14)

Creamy Chocolate Fudge Frosting (page 14)

1. Preheat the oven to 350°F. Coat the insides of three 8-inch cake pans with the 3 tablespoons butter and set aside.

2. In the bowl of an electric mixer, sift together the cake flour, sugar, and cocoa. Add the remaining ½ cup butter, the shortening, eggs, vanilla, buttermilk mixture, and milk. Using the electric mixer, beat at medium speed until the batter is smooth. Divide the batter equally among the prepared cake pans. Bake until the cake springs back when touched with your fingers, 35 to 40 minutes.

3. Remove from the oven and let cool in the pans for 8 to 10 minutes. Invert the cakes onto wire racks and let them cool completely.

4. Place the first layer upside down on a cake plate. Spread half of the filling almost to the outer edge with a flexible spatula. Place the second layer right side up on the filling. Spread the remaining filling almost to the outer edge. Place the third layer right side up on the filling. Spread the frosting evenly on the sides of the cake up to the top edge. Spread the frosting over the top, making attractive swirls with the spatula.

Chocolate Pecan Cake Filling

MAKES ENOUGH TO FILL ONE 3-LAYER CAKE

$1/4$ cup unsweetened cocoa powder

1 cup sugar

$1/4$ cup all-purpose flour

1 cup milk

$1/4$ cup light corn syrup

Pinch of salt

1 teaspoon pure vanilla extract

1 cup ground pecans

1. Combine the cocoa, sugar, and flour in a medium-size, heavy saucepan. Add the milk and stir until smooth. Add the corn syrup, salt, and vanilla and combine well.

2. Cook over medium-low heat, stirring constantly, until the mixture is smooth and thick. Remove from the heat and fold in the pecans. Let cool to room temperature before using.

Creamy Chocolate Fudge Frosting

MAKES ENOUGH TO FROST ONE 3-LAYER CAKE

$1/2$ cup unsweetened cocoa powder

2 cups sugar

One 8-ounce can evaporated milk

$1/4$ teaspoon salt

1 teaspoon pure vanilla extract

2 tablespoons butter

1. Combine the cocoa, sugar, evaporated milk, and salt in a large, heavy saucepan over medium heat. Cook, stirring often, until a little of the mixture dropped into cold water forms a soft ball, 234°F on a candy thermometer (see box).

2. Remove from the heat and let cool for a few minutes. Stir in the vanilla and butter and beat until it loses its gloss. Use immediately.

Cooking Sugar

When boiling sugar to make candy and syrups, there are tests that can be done by hand, if you don't have a candy thermometer, which is certainly the easiest and most reliable way to test. Eula Mae always has a cup of cold water and a spoon at hand when she begins the boiling process. When you think you're approaching the right temperature, test as follows:

Thread stage, 230°F: Drop a small spoonful of the boiling sugar syrup in the cold water. Knead the syrup between your index finger and thumb. It should form a thin thread when you separate your fingers from the syrup.

Soft-ball stage, 239°F: Drop a small spoonful of the boiling sugar syrup in the cold water. Knead the syrup between your index finger and thumb. It should form a soft ball on your finger.

Hard-ball stage, 248°F: Drop a small spoonful of the boiling sugar syrup in the cold water. Knead the syrup between your index finger and thumb. It should form a firm, pliable ball on your finger.

Soft-crack stage, 275°F: Drop a small spoonful of the boiling sugar syrup in the cold water. Knead the syrup between your index finger and thumb, then take a bite of it. It will be brittle but stick to your teeth.

Hard-crack stage, 295°F: Drop a small spoonful of the boiling sugar syrup in the cold water. Knead the syrup between your index finger and thumb, then take a bite of it. It will be very brittle and will not stick to your teeth.

MORNING-AFTER BRUNCH

Café au Lait

Eula Mae's Fig Preserves

Fried Boudin Balls

Pain Perdu

Marsh House Buttermilk Pancakes

Country Corn Cakes

Cream Cheese Scrambled Eggs

Creamy Cream Cheese Grits

Couche-Couche

Everybody works hard on the Island, and many play hard. A brunch or late breakfast is an ideal occasion to rehash the festivities of the night before and to enjoy a hearty meal.

"Breakfast, or brunch, is my favorite meal and I have developed some wonderful dishes that can really get your engines going after a long night! Most of these brunches are held at Marsh House, a lovely, rambling home that has one of the most impressive views of the surrounding area, since it's situated on a high ridge," explained Eula Mae one morning while she bustled around the kitchen.

The original house was built in 1818 for the Marsh family. In later years, another house was built nearby to accommodate the ever-growing families of the McIlhennys and Averys. It was usually referred to, appropriately, as "the Other House."

Around 1925, "the Other House" was razed to make way for a new Marsh House wing. In 1985 this wing was demolished by fire, but the old section was saved. A new section, complete with a large modern kitchen and a large dining room and sitting room, was added and now the home is ideal for family gatherings or for entertaining visitors.

A brunch or late breakfast is an ideal occasion to rehash the festivities of the night before and to enjoy a hearty meal.

Coffee milk, or *café au lait*, is nothing more than equal parts of hot coffee and hot milk or cream. New Orleanians prefer to use chicory coffee, but you rarely find chicory coffee in south Louisiana, where the locals like pure dark-roast coffee. Once the coffee and milk are poured into the cup, each person sweetens his own according to taste. And just a note here—in south Louisiana we always drink our coffee milk in large coffee cups with a saucer, not mugs. Here is a "recipe."

CAFÉ AU LAIT

MAKES ABOUT 8 CUPS (SERVINGS)

4 cups freshly brewed dark-roast coffee
4 cups hot (but not boiled) milk or cream

Pour equal amounts of coffee and milk into coffee cups. Pass the sugar for guests to sweeten the *café au lait* to taste.

The Celeste fig is what is primarily available in south Louisiana. Just about everyone has two or three fig trees in their yard. But Kadota figs can be canned as well.

"Our figs are at the peak around the Fourth of July. Then we have to watch that the blackbirds don't eat them up before we can pick them. The Celeste figs turn a wonderful purple color when they are still firm but ripe before they are picked. You'll never taste something as wonderful as these fig preserves. Put them on toast, pancakes, cornbread, or crackers for breakfast or as a snack."

Some people cut off the stems, but Eula Mae says to keep on a bit of the stems as it makes a better presentation. And by no means peel the figs.

EULA MAE'S FIG PRESERVES

MAKES ABOUT 6 PINTS

1 gallon ripe figs
8 cups sugar
2 cups water

1. Put the figs in a colander, rinse 2 to 3 times with cool water, and drain well.

2. Combine the sugar and water in a large, heavy pot and bring to a boil. Stir to dissolve the sugar and cook until a thick syrup forms. Add the figs and reduce the heat to medium. Simmer, uncovered, stirring occasionally, until the syrup is very thick and a foam appears around the edge of the pot, about 2 hours, depending on the size of the figs and the weather. It will take longer if the weather is hot and muggy. (Eula Mae says her test is to lift a spoonful of syrup out of the pot and let it drip out. When two drops meet at the rim of the spoon, it's ready.)

3. Spoon the hot mixture into sterilized preserving jars, filling to within ½ inch of the top. Wipe the jars and rims with a clean, damp towel. Fit with hot, sterilized lids. Tightly screw on the metal rings. Process in a hot water bath for 15 minutes. Remove from the heat and let the jars stand in the water until they are cool to the touch. Remove from the water and put on a towel on the counter and let cool completely.

4. Tighten the rings and store in a cool, dark place for up to 3 months. Refrigerate once opened.

Boudin (pronounced boo-danh) is a popular sausage in Acadiana. It's made with pork trimmings and rice, and flavored to perfection. You can find it in grocery stores, meat markets, or small convenience stores, and the locals like to wrap a slice of bread around it and eat it for breakfast, lunch, and mid-afternoon snacks.

Eula Mae, always trying to find a new way to present it to visitors, makes little patties or balls with the sausage mixture.

"I serve bacon, ham, sausage, and *boudin* at just about every breakfast and brunch on the Island," says Eula Mae.

FRIED BOUDIN BALLS

MAKES ABOUT 5 DOZEN

Eula Mae's Homemade Bread Crumbs (page 34), made with 8 slices rather than 10

1 large egg

$1/4$ teaspoon salt

$1/4$ teaspoon Tabasco brand pepper sauce

1 recipe Boudin Blanc (recipe follows)

4 cups peanut oil for deep-frying

1. Spread the bread crumbs evenly on large platter. In a shallow bowl, beat the egg with the salt and Tabasco.

2. Form balls about the size of a walnut with the *boudin* mixture. You should have about 5 dozen balls.

3. Heat the oil in a deep, heavy pot or an electric fryer to 360°F.

4. Dip the balls, in batches, in the egg mixture, then roll them in the bread crumbs, coating them evenly. Fry the balls, several at a time, in the hot oil until lightly browned, 3 to 4 minutes. Drain on paper towels. Serve warm.

VARIATION Alternately, the balls can be flattened into patties and fried in a little hot oil in a skillet.

Boudin is a mixture of bits of pork, rice, and seasonings stuffed into casings, thus resembling a sausage.

"When we used to have *boucheries*—hog slaughters—the ladies made *boudin* from the pork trimmings, because we always used everything from the pig except the squeal!"

Pork liver is available at most meat markets.

Boudin Blanc

MAKES ABOUT 3 QUARTS

5 pounds pork shoulder

1 pound pork liver, cleaned and coarsely chopped

4 large yellow onions, coarsely chopped

5 garlic cloves, peeled

2 cups long-grain white rice, cooked in 3 cups water with 1 teaspoon vinegar, 1 teaspoon
   vegetable oil, and a pinch of salt until all the water is absorbed (see page 171)

2 cups chopped green onions (green and white parts)

1 cup chopped fresh parsley leaves

1 teaspoon salt, or more to taste

¹/₄ teaspoon Tabasco brand pepper sauce

1. Put the pork shoulder and liver in a large, deep pot or Dutch oven. Add enough water to cover the meat and cook, covered, over medium heat until it is very tender, 1¹/₂ to 2 hours. Remove from the heat, drain, reserving the broth, and let cool.

2. Remove the meat from the bone and cut into 1-inch chunks. Cut the liver into 1-inch chunks. Put the pork, liver, onions, and garlic through the coarse grind die of a meat grinder. (Alternatively, it can be coarsely ground, in batches, in a food processor.) Combine this mixture with the cooked rice. Mix in the green onions and parsley. If the mixture is dry, add some of the reserved broth to moisten it. Season with the salt and Tabasco. This will keep refrigerated for up to 3 days. Do not freeze.

Pain perdu is French for "lost bread," since the bread usually used for making this dish was stale or day-old, the thrifty Acadians never letting anything go to waste. The ingredients are simple, but the result is fantastic.

"Try it, chère, and you'll see what I mean. When I can, I get honey from the beehives on the Island, or use cane syrup, but you can use regular honey or any kind of syrup."

PAIN PERDU

MAKES 4 TO 6 SERVINGS

4 large eggs, lightly beaten

1/2 cup milk

3 tablespoons granulated sugar

1 teaspoon pure vanilla extract

1/4 teaspoon ground ginger

1/8 teaspoon ground cinnamon

2 to 4 tablespoons butter

8 to 12 slices (each 1/2-inch-thick) day-old French bread or regular sliced bread

Confectioners' sugar

Honey

Syrup

1. Combine the eggs, milk, granulated sugar, vanilla, ginger, and cinnamon in a medium-size mixing bowl, and mix well.

2. Melt 2 tablespoons of the butter in a large skillet over medium-high heat.

3. Dip each bread slice into the batter, turning to coat evenly. Add 2 to 3 slices of the bread at a time to the skillet and fry until golden brown on both sides, turning once. Transfer to a warm platter and repeat the process with the remaining bread, adding more butter as needed.

4. Sprinkle with confectioners' sugar and serve warm with honey or syrup.

While I watched Eula Mae making these pancakes one day at Marsh House, I was amazed at her patience and charm. There were about twenty hungry guests waiting to be served brunch. But there she was, calmly and deftly flipping these pancakes, when one of the guests sauntered in and asked if he could watch her cook.

With a happy grin, she flipped one of the pancakes onto a small plate.

"Here you go! Do you want some butter and syrup?" she offered.

He sat down contentedly. As she cooked, she gave him one, then one went to the serving platter, and she repeated this until he finally had his fill.

MARSH HOUSE BUTTERMILK PANCAKES

MAKES ABOUT 1 DOZEN LARGE PANCAKES

2 cups cake flour

$\frac{1}{4}$ cup sugar

2 teaspoons baking powder

1 teaspoon salt

1 cup buttermilk

1 large egg

$\frac{1}{4}$ cup ($\frac{1}{2}$ stick) butter, melted

1. Sift the cake flour, sugar, baking powder, and salt together in a large mixing bowl.

2. In a medium-size mixing bowl, mix together the buttermilk, egg, and melted butter. Add this to the dry mixture and mix to a light batter consistency.

3. Lightly brush a large skillet or griddle with vegetable oil. Spoon the batter, about 2 tablespoons at a time (or more if you wish large pancakes), onto the hot surface, and cook until tiny bubbles begin to appear all over the surface, about $1\frac{1}{2}$ minutes. Then, with a metal spatula, turn and cook the other side until golden, 30 to 40 seconds. When they are browned on both sides, transfer to a platter. Lightly brush the skillet again if necessary with vegetable oil and repeat the process until all the batter is used.

"These are very much like regular pancakes, but the cornmeal gives these a little coarser texture. Because they are denser and firmer, I've seen guests sprinkle them with sugar, add fig or strawberry preserves, and roll them up before eating them!"

COUNTRY CORN CAKES

MAKES ABOUT 1 DOZEN

2 large eggs

1 cup milk

$^1/_2$ cup yellow cornmeal

$^1/_2$ cup all-purpose flour

$^1/_2$ teaspoon salt

1 teaspoon baking powder

$^1/_2$ cup vegetable shortening, melted

1. Combine the eggs and milk in a medium-size mixing bowl and whisk to blend. In a small mixing bowl, sift the cornmeal, flour, salt, and baking powder together. Stir the dry mixture into the wet mixture until well combined.

2. Lightly brush a large skillet or griddle with shortening. Spoon the batter, about 2 table-spoons at a time (or more if you wish large pancakes), and cook until tiny bubbles begin to appear all over the surface, 2 to 3 minutes. Then, with a metal spatula, turn and cook the other side. When they are browned on both sides, transfer to a platter. Lightly brush the skillet again with shortening if necessary and repeat the process until all the batter is used.

When Eula Mae lived on the family farm with her father and siblings, there were plenty of fresh yard eggs from the chickens they raised.

"Eggs were mainly for breakfast, but sometimes we fixed a simple meal by frying some bits of bacon or ham with green onions and leftover rice, then stirred in a few lightly beaten eggs," Eula Mae recalls. "Darling, this fried rice dish accompanied by buttered cornbread was quite a feast back then."

When there is a crowd for breakfast, this is a favorite preparation on the Island. Eula Mae has perfected this dish in the microwave to save time.

"Well, sometimes those new kitchen appliances come in handy. I usually have to make two or three batches for large groups. I can tell you that this dish will make your head and tummy feel a lot better after a long night of partying."

CREAM CHEESE SCRAMBLED EGGS

MAKES ABOUT 12 SERVINGS

16 jumbo eggs

One 8-ounce package cream cheese, at room temperature

1 teaspoon Tabasco brand pepper sauce

$1/2$ teaspoon salt

$1/4$ teaspoon Accent seasoning

$1/4$ teaspoon freshly ground black pepper

2 cups milk

1. Combine all the ingredients in a large glass microwave-safe bowl. Stir well to blend. Put into the microwave and cook for 2 minutes.

2. Remove from the microwave and stir the mixture. Return to the microwave for another minute or two, and repeat the process until the mixture is set but is still moist. This should take about 8 minutes. The cooking time will vary according to the intensity of the heat setting on the microwave. Serve hot.

Grits, for those of you not familiar with them, are simply finely ground corn. They can be cooked with boiling water or milk, and you can add cheese, eggs, and butter to make an even richer dish.

"Hot, creamy grits will cure anything that ails you. There are many guests that have told me that they have never had grits before. And I tell them, they will want to take this recipe so that they can fix this at home! It's a good breakfast dish, but you certainly can serve it anytime."

CREAMY CREAM CHEESE GRITS

MAKES ABOUT 12 SERVINGS

1 quart milk

$1/4$ teaspoon garlic powder

1 teaspoon salt

$1/4$ teaspoon white pepper

$1/4$ teaspoon Tabasco brand pepper sauce

1 cup white quick-cooking grits

4 ounces cream cheese, cut into cubes

4 ounces American or Cheddar cheese, cut into cubes

1. In a large saucepan over medium-high heat, combine the milk, garlic powder, salt, white pepper, and Tabasco. Heat, stirring slowly and constantly, until the milk just comes to a boil. Add the grits and stir to mix. Reduce the heat to low, cover, and cook until the mixture is thick and creamy, 5 to 6 minutes.

2. Add the cheeses and stir until they melt completely. Serve warm.

NOTE If there's any left over, pour it into a small shallow square dish. After it has been refrigerated, you can cut it into squares and pour cold milk over them.

Not to be confused with *couscous*, a staple of North African cuisine, this is a thick cereal-type dish that's a Cajun breakfast specialty. "Some like it served with hot *café au lait* (coffee milk), while others like to drench the mixture with cane syrup. Still others like to top it with a fried egg sprinkled with salt and black pepper. You'll have to try all the ways yourself, then decide which one you like best, *oui*."

COUCHE-COUCHE

MAKES 4 TO 6 SERVINGS

1 cup yellow cornmeal

¾ cup water

1 teaspoon salt

1 tablespoon vegetable oil

1. In a medium-size mixing bowl, combine the cornmeal, water, and salt. Stir well to mix.

2. Heat the oil over medium heat in a heavy skillet, preferably cast iron, and fry the mixture while stirring continuously. The mixture will form a light crust as you cook. Scrape the bottom of the pot clean every time you stir and fold the crust over the mixture. It will be crumbly. Serve hot.

EASTER ON THE CHÊNIÈRE

Hot Tamales

Crawfish Bisque

Lemon Fluff

Blackberry Dumplings

"When I was a little girl, Easter was celebrated with a big family dinner that usually included baked or fricasseed chicken, or maybe a roasted goose. On the day before Easter, we spent most of the afternoon dying Easter eggs. We always had plenty of yard eggs from our chickens."

The dyes were homemade. Coffee grinds, yellow onion skins, and spinach were used to color the water in which the eggs were dipped. Also, colored fabrics were wrapped around the eggs, which were then dipped in boiling water. The color, or pattern, of the fabric transferred to the eggs.

"The eggs were hidden around the yard by the older children. We used a large goose egg for the golden or prize egg. We made do with whatever we had."

These days, Eula Mae has a few chickens but not nearly enough to supply her the amount of eggs needed for a big hunt.

"Well, *chère*, there aren't as many children around to have a hunt and our traditions for celebrating Easter have changed. Everybody on the Island celebrates Easter differently," says Eula Mae. "Some of the families get together for a crawfish boil and others may have a barbecue after the Easter Sunday Mass. For years, my family and I have gone to the *chênière*, a place where we have a camp." Just about everyone in south Louisiana has a "camp," which can be anything from a humble trapper's cabin to a spacious, comfortable second home with all the modern conveniences.

Along the southwestern fringe of Louisiana, there's a constant struggle between earth and water. As the Mississippi River was building its westernmost subdeltas, some of the sediment it carried washed out to sea and was carried farther west by Gulf currents. During storms, the sediment piled onto beaches in ridges that paralleled the shore. The ridges slowly formed barricades of mud, silt, and shells where plants grow safe from the water. The ridges are called *chênières*, from the French *chêne*, meaning oak, because they are places where live oaks flourish. The clinging roots of the trees help to hold the lands fast against the battering waves.

Eula Mae's family has been going to their place on the *chênière* for years and especially for the Easter holiday. The camp is a simple but comfortable cottage that was constructed under several graceful oaks. The adjoining pastures are green and lush during the spring.

"It's always so peaceful there and it's a special place for my family and me to gather together," says Eula Mae. "We can hunt, fish, and crab in the marsh, so much of what we eat is what we catch. We always have food, good food!"

They leave on Thursday or Friday and stay until Easter Sunday. There are so many—aunts, uncles, cousins, friends—that some sleep on thick quilts on the floor. There might be as many as twenty people staying at the cottage over the holiday.

"Oh, *chère*, we have so much fun being together and we are always cooking!"

"It's always so peaceful there and it's a special place for my family and me to gather together."

When Eula Mae was a young girl, she sometimes would go to a movie in New Iberia, then stop by a place called Walet's on Hopkins Street to get a dozen tamales to share with her father.

"He loved them so much, I was determined to learn how to make them just like Walet's did. I studied those tamales and would you believe I was successful? It wasn't easy, but I dissected the tamales, tried different cuts of pork and different seasonings until I got it right! Now, when I go with my family to the *chênière*, we get together and make several batches of tamales. They freeze well, so we can have them all year long."

Tamales are not usual Cajun fare, but these are so good Eula Mae said she wanted to include them here.

Eula Mae's daughter, Susan, explains that they often make the tamales at the *chênière* "because we like cooking together and this is one of the times during the year that our family is all together. Sometimes I ask Mama to show us how to make one of her dishes, like gumbo, jambalaya, or a cake, so that we can watch her firsthand. That's how we learn her recipes and her techniques to keep them in the family."

Masa harina is simply corn flour and is available in many supermarkets or Latin markets. Eula Mae prefers using paper tamale wrappers rather than the dried corn husks because they are easier to work with. The paper wrappers are available in many supermarkets and Latin markets.

HOT TAMALES

MAKES 4 TO 5 DOZEN

1 pork shoulder, about 3 pounds

One 3-pound beef brisket

One 10-ounce can diced tomatoes with green chiles

2 medium-size yellow onions, peeled

5 garlic cloves, peeled

1 medium-size red bell pepper, cut in half and seeded

1 tablespoon sweet paprika

3 tablespoons salt

7 tablespoons chili powder

2 tablespoons Tabasco brand pepper sauce

4 quarts water

2 pounds masa harina flour (corn flour)

4 to 5 dozen paper tamale wrappers, moistened with water

1. Put the pork shoulder, brisket, tomatoes with chiles, onions, garlic, bell pepper, paprika, 1 tablespoon of the salt, 3 tablespoons of the chili powder, and 1 tablespoon of the Tabasco in a large pot with the water. Cover and cook over medium heat until the meat is very tender, about 3 hours. Transfer the meat to a platter and let cool. Strain the broth and set aside.

2. When the meat is cool, grind it coarsely in a meat grinder or food processor. Do not puree or overprocess. Season the meat mixture with 1 tablespoon of the salt, 3 tablespoons of the chili powder, and the remaining 1 tablespoon Tabasco. Mix well and set aside.

3. Combine the masa harina, the remaining 1 tablespoon salt and the remaining 1 tablespoon chili powder in a large mixing bowl. Take the congealed fat that rises to the surface of the broth and about 1 cup of the broth, add it to the flour mixture, and mix. Add more broth if necessary to make a mush, like a soft paste.

4. Take a moistened tamale wrapper and lay it flat on a work surface. Put 1 tablespoon of the mush on the wrapper and spread it evenly over the upper third of the paper. Put 2 tablespoons of the meat mixture over the mush and spread it evenly. Gently roll the tamale paper to encase the mush-and-meat mixture evenly and smoothly. Then roll the wrapper around it to make a roll 5 inches long and 1 inch in diameter. (Use your hands—they are the best tools.) Tuck in the ends. Repeat the process until all the mush-and-meat mixture is used.

5. Layer the tamales in a deep, heavy pot, large enough to accommodate all the tamales in several layers. Pour enough of the reserved broth almost to cover, about 8 cups. Cover the pot, and simmer over medium-low heat, basting the top occasionally with the broth, until the tamales can be removed from the papers without sticking, about 1 hour and 15 minutes.

6. Remove from the heat. Skim off any fat that rises to the surface by blotting it away with paper towels. Serve warm on plates.

NOTE To freeze, put the tamales after they are cooked in plastic storage bags with a little of the broth to keep them moist. They'll keep frozen for 3 to 4 months. They can be reheated in the microwave, or placed in a shallow baking pan with the broth, covered with aluminum foil, and heated slowly in a preheated 250°F oven.

Eula Mae often prepares crawfish bisque at Easter, since the crawfish are in season (January through June) and it's another dish the family can make together.

"I never let the season go by without making crawfish bisque," says Eula Mae. "It takes the better part of the day to prepare, but when the family is all together at Easter, the work goes faster with the extra hands. And we have so much fun doing this that we make several batches. If it isn't all eaten while we're at the camp, it can be frozen. But, *chère*, it isn't often there is anything left."

The Cajuns have always been both creative and innovative, always trying to do something different with whatever local ingredients they have on hand. This bisque, in which the heads are stuffed with ground crawfish tails combined with some bread crumbs to bind the mixture, then cooked in a rich, stew-like sauce, is yet another preparation for the local crawfish.

"It goes to show you that when something is prepared with lots of love, it's appreciated. Oh, and be sure to have lots of crusty French bread to accompany the meal," Eula Mae reminds us.

CRAWFISH BISQUE

MAKES 8 SERVINGS

10 pounds live crawfish

1 cup plus 3 tablespoons vegetable oil

1 cup all-purpose flour

1 tablespoon tomato paste

2 cups chopped yellow onions

$1^{1}/_{2}$ cups seeded and chopped green bell peppers

1 cup chopped celery

3 garlic cloves, peeled

2 quarts warm water

$1^{1}/_{2}$ teaspoons salt

$^{1}/_{2}$ teaspoon cayenne

1 cup Eula Mae's Homemade Bread Crumbs (page 34)

1 large egg, lightly beaten

$^{1}/_{4}$ cup chopped green onions (green and white parts)

$^{1}/_{4}$ cup chopped fresh flat-leaf parsley leaves

1. Rinse the crawfish under cool tap water. Discard any that are dead (you can tell because the tail is straight, not curled). Bring a large pot (large enough to accommodate the crawfish) of water to a boil. Add the crawfish and boil until they turn bright red, about 10 minutes. Drain well and let cool.

2. When cool, remove the head section from the tail. Gently tap the heads on the rim of a bowl to remove the fat. Trim the eyes of the head section away with a knife or kitchen shears. Rinse the heads with cool tap water and drain well. Set them on a sheet pan lined with aluminum foil to dry. Peel the tails and devein. Divide the tails; you will need 2 cups for the stuffing and the rest will go into the bisque.

3. Heat 1 cup of the oil in a large, heavy pot or Dutch oven over medium heat. Add ¾ cup of the flour and, stirring slowly and constantly, make a roux the color of peanut butter (see page 94 for Eula Mae's advice on making a roux). Add the tomato paste and stir to blend. Add 1½ cups of the chopped onions, 1 cup of the bell peppers, ½ cup of the celery, and 2 of the garlic cloves. Cook, stirring, until the vegetables are very soft, about 10 minutes. Add the warm water and stir to blend. Reduce the heat to medium-low and simmer, stirring occasionally, for 30 minutes. Add all but the reserved 2 cups of the crawfish tails and season with 1 teaspoon of the salt and ¼ teaspoon of the cayenne.

4. Coarsely chop the remaining 2 cups crawfish tails and set aside.

5. Heat the remaining 3 tablespoons oil in a saucepan over medium heat. Add the remaining ½ cup chopped onions, ½ cup chopped bell peppers, ½ cup chopped celery, and garlic clove and cook, stirring, until soft, about 8 minutes. Add the bread crumbs and chopped crawfish tails. Season with the remaining ½ teaspoon salt and ¼ teaspoon cayenne. (You may want to add more seasoning—you have to taste it.) Remove from the heat and stir in the beaten egg to bind the stuffing.

6. Preheat the oven to 350°F.

7. Stuff each crawfish head with a tablespoon or two of the stuffing and return the heads to the sheet pan. Bake for 20 minutes.

8. Add the baked crawfish heads to the bisque, along with the green onions and parsley. Stir gently and simmer for 2 to 3 minutes. Adjust the seasoning if necessary.

9. Serve hot in gumbo or soup bowls. The stuffing can be removed from the heads with a fork.

One day when Eula Mae and I were cooking in the test kitchen, she pulled out her old blender. I laughed because I know how she is about new-fangled gadgets and kitchen equipment.

"Today I'm going to show you how to make fresh bread crumbs. I refuse to buy bread crumbs in the supermarkets. Darling, they are so easy to make and one always has bread on hand," she explained. "And you can use fresh or day-old bread to do this. The bread doesn't have to be day-old or stale. Use whatever you have on hand. In the old days, we had homemade bread that was rather coarse. When it got stale, we would grate the bread to make bread crumbs.

"I do two kinds of bread crumbs because I don't want to waste. Remove the crusts from regular sliced white bread. These will make bread crumbs to sprinkle on top of casseroles when you want a pretty brown color and, of course, they are a little coarser.

"The crumbs made with the white bread are for other things, like breading or to bind mixtures.

"When I was younger, we couldn't just run into town, so we always tried to make do with what we had on hand."

Eula Mae's Homemade Bread Crumbs

MAKES ABOUT 2 CUPS WHITE BREAD CRUMBS
AND ABOUT 1 CUP CRUST BREAD CRUMBS

10 slices plain white bread, crusts trimmed and reserved

1. Cut each slice of bread into quarters. Put several at a time in a blender. Pulse two or three times, then remove and shake the blender container. Continue pulsing on "crumb" until the bread is fine and looks like freshly grated Parmesan cheese. Repeat the process with the crusts.

2. Transfer the crumbs to separate airtight containers and refrigerate or freeze. They will keep for several days in the refrigerator and 2 to 3 months in the freezer.

"In my opinion, Easter calls for a special dessert. This is ideal for our Easter celebration because it's rich, pretty, and lemony—what I like to cleanse the palate after the crawfish bisque. I usually use My Pound Cake for this dessert, but sometimes, when I can find good ladyfingers at the local bakery, I'll use them. What you must always remember is that desserts need to be pretty. Ladies and, yes, gentlemen, like pretty things. You want to make sure everything looks nice for guests. The filling in this dish simply disappears in your mouth. And be sure to use only fresh lemon juice. A friend made this recipe and called to tell me that it just didn't taste like mine. Well, no, it didn't, she had used that bottled juice! Take the time to squeeze fresh lemons—it really does make a difference."

LEMON FLUFF

MAKES ABOUT 8 SERVINGS

1 recipe My Pound Cake (page 36)
4 large eggs, separated
1 cup granulated sugar
6 tablespoons fresh lemon juice
2 teaspoons grated lemon zest
One $\frac{1}{4}$-ounce envelope gelatin dissolved in $\frac{1}{4}$ cup water
1 cup heavy cream
$\frac{1}{4}$ cup confectioners' sugar
1 teaspoon pure vanilla extract

1. Cut the pound cake into $\frac{1}{4}$-inch-thick slices. Line the bottom and sides of a deep glass bowl or shallow platter with the cake. Set aside.

2. Combine the egg yolks with $\frac{1}{4}$ cup of the granulated sugar in the top of a double boiler set over simmering water, stirring until the sugar dissolves. Add the lemon juice and continue to stir until the mixture is smooth. Add the lemon zest and continue to whisk until the mixture is thick enough to coat the back of a spoon, about 5 minutes. Add the gelatin mixture and whisk until it thickens and is smooth. Remove from the heat and let cool completely.

3. In a large mixing bowl, using an electric mixture, beat the egg whites with the remaining $\frac{1}{2}$ cup granulated sugar until glossy and stiff peaks form. Fold the lemon mixture, a little at a time, slowly and gently into the meringue. Pour the mixture over the pound cake in the bowl. Wash and dry the mixer beaters.

4. In a medium-size mixing bowl, using an electric mixer, beat the heavy cream, confectioners' sugar, and vanilla together until soft peaks form. Spread the cream mixture over the top of the custard with a rubber spatula, then cover loosely with plastic wrap and chill for at least 8 hours before serving.

5. To serve, cut into wedges.

Eula Mae claims that it's best not to have a pound cake that is too sweet, since everything else she serves with it will be sweet. Sometimes she makes small ones, but then again, she sometimes makes a one-pound loaf. One can tell she has made hundreds, if not thousands, of pound cakes by the well-worn pans in her tidy kitchen. This is the pound cake she uses to make Lemon Fluff (page 35) and Charlotte Russe (page 68), but it can also be served simply with fresh berries or ice cream.

My Pound Cake

MAKES 1 LARGE LOAF OR 3 SMALL ONES

1 cup (2 sticks) butter, at room temperature

1 cup sugar

5 large eggs, separated

1 teaspoon pure vanilla extract

2 cups cake flour

$1/2$ teaspoon baking powder

$1/4$ teaspoon ground mace

$1/8$ teaspoon salt

1. Preheat the oven to 300°F. Lightly oil an 8 $1/2$ x 4 $1/2$ x 2 $1/2$-inch loaf pan, 3 smaller loaf pans, or a Bundt pan.

2. Beat the butter in a large mixing bowl with an electric mixer until fluffy. Gradually add the sugar, beating on low speed until the mixture is thick and creamy. Add the egg yolks, one at a time, beating well after each addition. Stir in the vanilla.

3. In a medium-size mixing bowl, sift together the cake flour, baking powder, mace, and salt. Add this mixture, about 3 tablespoons at a time, to the sugar-and-egg mixture, beating after each addition until the batter is thick and smooth.

4. In another large mixing bowl, using an electric mixer, beat the egg whites until soft peaks form. Gently fold the egg whites, about 1 cup at a time, using a rubber spatula, into the batter until the mixture is smooth.

5. Pour the batter into the large loaf pan and bake until golden and the center rises in a peak and springs back when touched, about 1 hour. (Alternately, bake the small ones until golden and the center rises in a peak, about 50 minutes.)

6. Remove from the oven and let cool for 3 to 4 minutes, then turn out of the pan onto a wire rack to cool completely.

During the spring, Eula Mae is very attentive to the blackberry bushes that flourish on the Island. I went picking with her one spring morning while the dew was still on the berries. She was crowing with delight, pointing here and there so I wouldn't miss any. We popped a few in our mouths as we walked back to her home. We discussed all the possibilities of preparing them, but Eula Mae insisted that we make these dumplings, which are a favorite of both children and adults.

"That's why I like to make them when the family gathers at the camp."

It's always best to use fresh blackberries but you can use frozen in a pinch. Reserve a few fresh berries to use as garnish when serving the dumplings with homemade ice cream. The main thing is to take your time. Do not flip the dumplings until they are bubbly like pancakes. Don't hurry!

BLACKBERRY DUMPLINGS

MAKES ABOUT 35 DUMPLINGS OR 8 SERVINGS

1 pound fresh blackberries, rinsed and picked over, or 1 pound frozen blackberries, thawed

1 cup sugar

1 cup all-purpose flour

1 cup yellow butter cake mix

1 teaspoon baking powder

1 large egg beaten with $1/2$ cup water

Vanilla ice cream

1. Combine the berries and the sugar in a heavy, medium-size saucepan over medium heat. Cook, stirring occasionally, for 15 minutes. Reduce the heat to medium-low.

2. Meanwhile, combine the flour, cake mix, and baking powder in a medium-size mixing bowl and mix well. Make a well in the center of the dry ingredients and pour in the egg-water mixture. With a wooden spoon, stir in one direction to make a smooth dough.

3. Drop the batter randomly by heaping teaspoonfuls into the hot blackberries, 6 to 7 teaspoonfuls at a time. Poach for about 2 minutes, then carefully and gently flip over the batter with the tines of a fork. Cook until the dumplings are puffy and spongy, 1 to 2 minutes longer. Gently transfer them to a shallow bowl. Repeat with the remaining batter.

4. To serve, spoon an equal amount of the remaining blackberry mixture from the pot into the bottom of each small dessert bowl. Put four dumplings in the bowl on top of the blackberry sauce, then top with a scoop of ice cream and garnish with the fresh berries or some of the cooked blackberry mixture.

MAY WEDDING

Fried Eggplant Rounds

Fried Crawfish Tails

Bayou Petite Anse Crab Mold

Tried and True Shrimp Mold

Finger Sandwiches

Wild Game Jambalaya

Party Pecan Tarts

Celebration Strawberry Shortcake

Traditional Acadian, or Cajun, weddings were very simple affairs. Of course, most of the brides had white dresses and veils when they entered the church. Yes, there was food, plenty of it, after the wedding ceremony, but it was nothing fancy. There might have been a huge pot of jambalaya and one of gumbo, chicken salad sandwiches, or barbecued chicken served with rice dressing. And there was always a long table on which numerous homemade cakes were presented. A Cajun band, likely as not, provided the music. The rhythmic chank-a-chank music came from an accordion, perhaps a fiddle, and a triangle. Anyone who wanted to dance with the bride had to pay for that dance by pinning bills to her veil and dress. The money came in handy either for a brief honeymoon or to furnish the newlyweds' new home.

Today, the tradition continues, but only in the most rural areas of Acadiana. Now the more affluent descendants of the Acadians have a "big" wedding, replete with a large reception and, again, plenty of food, although the food now may be a bit fancier.

Susan, Eula Mae's daughter, had such a wedding.

"It was held on Jefferson Island, not far from Avery Island. It's a beautiful place and the ceremony was held at sunset, on the lawn overlooking Lake Pegnieur."

The reception following the ceremony was staged in a nearby building.

"Of course, guests, about three hundred, meandered by the lake, going in and out of the building, and munching on crab dip, fried chicken wings, assorted finger sandwiches, and boiled shrimp with cocktail sauce," Susan says. "We gave Mama a break so she could enjoy the wedding. As far as I was concerned, the highlight of the food was the wedding cake—Amaretto pecan and double chocolate cheesecake! We didn't have any left. We also had mini chocolate éclairs and cream puffs. It was a grand evening, with lots of dancing and good food."

Eula Mae has helped prepare and serve for just about all of the McIlhenny weddings on Avery Island. Most of the ceremonies have been held under the canopy of giant oak trees near Marsh House, the large, rambling edifice that is often used by the families for large affairs.

"We serve just about everything buffet style and pass finger food on trays."

The house, with wide verandas and large, comfortable rooms, is ideal for a May wedding. The kitchen is equipped with stoves, ovens, refrigerators, and more than adequate work areas.

"It's delightful to work in that kitchen," says Eula Mae.

More often than not, there's a band to provide music to which guests can dance on a dance floor set up under the trees. Decorating for the weddings and receptions is minimal. The azaleas, magnolias, irises, and ferns that grow practically wild all over the Island provide blossoms and greenery to arrange in huge urns in the main rooms of Marsh House.

And the view, well, it is nothing short of majestic. One can see out to the marshes and the wooded areas in the distance are luxuriant. The sunsets are spectacular. The air is filled with the scent of jasmine, honeysuckle, and gardenias.

"Because there is usually a large crowd, we serve just about everything buffet style and pass finger food on trays. It takes a couple of weeks to get all the food prepared and stored, and in a matter of a couple of hours, it's all gone! But it always makes me happy to know that the food was good and people enjoyed themselves!"

Eggplant is quite common in the home gardens on the Island during the spring and summer months. The Cajuns, both thrifty and creative, have long prepared eggplant in various ways—cut into *bâtons* (sticks) or rounds, combined with rice for dressings and stuffings, and baked with cheese and bread crumbs.

"I usually have some green-skinned ones and they are ideal for preparing this dish," says Eula Mae.

Serve them on platters with Tartar Sauce (page 193) for passing around.

FRIED EGGPLANT ROUNDS

MAKES ABOUT 6 SERVINGS (2 SLICES PER PERSON)

3 medium-size green eggplant, cut crosswise into $^1/_4$-inch-thick slices

3 cups water

3 teaspoons salt

2 cups Zatarain's Wonderful Fish-Fri (see Source Guide, page 223)

$^1/_2$ teaspoon cayenne

$^1/_2$ teaspoon freshly ground black pepper

3 to 4 cups peanut oil for deep-frying

1. Soak the eggplant slices in the water seasoned with 2 teaspoons of the salt for about 1 hour. Drain, rinse with cool water, and pat dry.

2. Season the Zatarain's with the remaining 1 teaspoon salt, the cayenne, and black pepper in a medium-size mixing bowl.

3. Heat the oil in a large, deep pot or an electric fryer to 360°F. When it's hot, dredge the eggplant, several at a time, in the Zatarain's mixture. Carefully place 3 or 4 slices at a time in the hot oil and fry until golden, about 3 minutes. Remove from the oil with a slotted spoon, drain on paper towels, and serve immediately with tartar sauce. (Do not attempt to keep these hot in the oven; they'll just become soggy.)

You'll often hear the locals call this "popcorn" crawfish because you can just pop them in your mouth right after they're cooked and eat them like popcorn. You might want to double or triple the recipe because people go crazy over them!

"Crawfish are so versatile and these fried tails are perfect for wedding receptions and cocktail parties. I call them 'finger food' because guests can pick them up and dab them in tartar sauce or remoulade sauce."

The locals like to shake crawfish, shrimp, chicken, and catfish in a brown paper bag in which they put the breading mixture.

"This is so much easier and neater than dredging them one by one, especially when you have a crowd and there's a large amount of food to fry," says Eula Mae.

FRIED CRAWFISH TAILS

MAKES 6 TO 8 APPETIZER SERVINGS

1 pound peeled crawfish tails

$1/2$ cup buttermilk

1 large egg white, beaten until slightly foamy

1 teaspoon salt

$1/4$ teaspoon Tabasco brand pepper sauce

$1^1/2$ cups Eula Mae's Homemade Bread Crumbs (white; page 34)

4 cups peanut oil for deep-frying

Tartar Sauce (page 193) or Remoulade Sauce (page 44)

1. Combine the crawfish tails, buttermilk, egg white, salt, and Tabasco in a medium-size mixing bowl. Toss to coat evenly and let sit for about 10 minutes.

2. Put the bread crumbs in a large brown paper bag.

3. Heat the oil in a large, heavy pot or electric fryer to 360°F. When it's hot, put the crawfish tails in the bag with the bread crumbs and shake to coat evenly. Fry the crawfish tails, 6 to 8 at a time, in the hot oil until they are lightly golden, about 3 minutes. Remove from the oil with a slotted spoon, drain on paper towels, and serve immediately with the tartar or remoulade sauce on the side.

Remoulade sauce has its origin in France, so when the early French settlers arrived in New Orleans, they quickly realized that it was ideal to serve with local seafood, boiled, fried, or baked.

"When I was learning to cook many years ago, I experimented with different ingredients for my remoulade. A few drops of Tabasco sauce really bring out the flavor. You might think it would overpower the delicate taste of seafood, but *non*, it gives it a little smack! That's the taste we like!"

Most remoulades made in Louisiana do not contain any mayonnaise. A hot, tart, pungent sauce is preferred; however, if you wish, you can add a tablespoon or two of mayonnaise to this mixture to take out the "bite."

Creole mustard is made with spicy brown mustard seeds. The seeds are steeped in vinegar and then coarsely ground. You can substitute any whole-grain brown mustard if you wish.

Remoulade Sauce

MAKES ABOUT 2 $^1/_2$ CUPS

$^1/_2$ cup Creole mustard or any whole-grain mustard

1 cup salad oil

$^1/_2$ cup distilled white vinegar

1 teaspoon Tabasco brand pepper sauce

1 teaspoon freshly ground black pepper

1 teaspoon salt

$^1/_4$ cup grated onions

2 tablespoons minced fresh parsley leaves

1 cup finely chopped celery

1. Combine all the ingredients in a bowl and whisk to blend well.

2. Cover and refrigerate for 1 hour before serving. The sauce will keep in the refrigerator for up to 3 days.

As you arrive at Avery Island, you must travel over a small bridge over Bayou Petite Anse. During the spring and summer, men, women, and children from the Island gather early in the mornings, before the heat of the day sets in, and again late in the afternoons, when the sun begins its descent into the western sky, to fish and crab from the bridge.

The crab nets, baited with chicken necks, are lowered into the still, green-gray water. The nets are then tied to the posts on the bridge. And then one waits a while. Within a few minutes, the crab nets are pulled slowly up and, with luck, each will hold several blue crabs. In no time at all, the crabbers will have all they need for supper.

"I can't tell you how many crabs I've caught!" said Eula Mae with a laugh one day while we were walking on the Island. "Of course, we like to boil them. But sometimes we have so much, I scald and peel them to use in other preparations, like this crab mold."

Nothing is ever wasted and the bounty from the many waterways that criss-cross the southern section of the state is always appreciated.

This mold goes a long way at cocktail parties and receptions. Make sure you use fresh, fresh crabmeat.

BAYOU PETITE ANSE CRAB MOLD

MAKES ABOUT 50 APPETIZER SERVINGS

One 10 3/4-ounce can Campbell's condensed cream of mushroom soup

Two 1/4-ounce envelopes gelatin dissolved in 1/2 cup water

One 8-ounce package cream cheese, at room temperature

1 cup mayonnaise

1 teaspoon Tabasco brand pepper sauce

1 teaspoon salt

1 teaspoon white pepper

1/2 cup chopped green onions (green and white parts)

1/2 cup chopped fresh parsley leaves

1 pound white crabmeat, picked over for shells and cartilage

Several sprigs fresh parsley

1. Heat the soup over medium heat in a large saucepan. Add the gelatin mixture and stir until smooth. Add the cream cheese, mayonnaise, Tabasco, salt, white pepper, green onions, and parsley. Stir to mix. Add the crabmeat and stir gently to blend.

2. Pour into a decorative mold lightly coated with mayonnaise, let cool a bit, cover, and refrigerate until the mixture sets, about 3 hours.

3. To serve, unmold onto a serving platter. Garnish with the parsley sprigs and serve with toast points or party crackers.

This shrimp mold has been a popular item to serve at wedding receptions, cocktail parties, ladies' teas, and bridal showers for over fifty years on the Island. It's one of Eula Mae's tried and true recipes that has been passed down from generation to generation.

"Well, *chère*, we have fresh shrimp from the bays and the Gulf and they are so sweet and succulent, it would be a shame not to use them," she told me one day while we boiled and peeled pounds of shrimp to make several of these molds for a wedding.

The mixture can be put into decorative molds, but you can also use deep glass dishes as well. When ready to serve, garnish them with pretty fresh parsley sprigs and decorate the platter with olives and cocktail onions.

TRIED AND TRUE SHRIMP MOLD

MAKES ABOUT 75 APPETIZER SERVINGS

1 tablespoon vegetable oil

$^1/_4$ cup finely chopped onions

$^1/_2$ cup finely chopped celery

One 10$^3/_4$-ounce can Campbell's condensed tomato soup

$^1/_2$ cup water

One 8-ounce package cream cheese, cut into bits

2 pounds boiled shrimp, peeled and coarsely ground or chopped

1 cup plus 1 tablespoon mayonnaise

$^1/_2$ teaspoon salt

2 teaspoons Tabasco brand pepper sauce

Two $^1/_4$-ounce envelopes gelatin dissolved in $^1/_2$ cup water

Several sprigs fresh parsley

1. Heat the oil over medium heat in a medium-size skillet. Add the onions and celery and cook, stirring, until slightly soft, about 3 minutes. Remove from the heat and drain on paper towels. Set aside.

2. Combine the tomato soup and water in a large, heavy saucepan over medium-low heat. Stir to blend and bring to a gentle boil. Add the cream cheese and stir until it is completely melted.

Add the shrimp, the reserved onions and celery, and 1 cup of the mayonnaise. Add the salt and Tabasco. Mix well. Add the gelatin mixture and stir until smooth.

3. Lightly grease a 2-quart decorative mold with the remaining 1 tablespoon mayonnaise. Pour the mixture into the mold and let cool for about 15 minutes. Cover and refrigerate until it sets, at least 3 hours.

4. When ready to serve, unmold and arrange on a serving platter. Garnish with the parsley sprigs. Serve with toast points or party crackers.

Simple finger sandwiches are *de rigueur* at most weddings in south Louisiana.

"It just wouldn't be a wedding without these little sandwiches," says Eula Mae. "They are easy to make and you can use all sorts of things for fillings. Years ago, we made dainty bread pinwheels filled with flavored cream cheese, but that is so time consuming."

Here are some pointers from Eula Mae for making perfect finger sandwiches:

You can use thin slices of white and/or whole wheat bread. It's best that the bread is neither too fresh nor too soft, so that it is easily cut. Use an electric knife to cut the bread—it's easier and cuts the preparation time in half. Spread a slice of bread with the filling, making sure to cover the entire surface. Top with another slice of bread. You can use one slice of white and top with one slice of wheat, or whatever. Trim the crusts, then cut the sandwiches into "points" or "squares." Thus, each sandwich will make four finger sandwiches. As you work, arrange the sandwiches closely together on trays or sheet pans and cover with a lightly dampened, clean towel or plastic wrap to keep them from drying out. They can be refrigerated, covered with a damp towel or plastic wrap, for as long as four hours before serving.

FINGER SANDWICHES
40 THIN SLICES BREAD OF CHOICE = 80 FINGER SANDWICHES

Cheddar Cheese Filling
MAKES ABOUT 2 CUPS, ENOUGH FOR ABOUT 80 FINGER SANDWICHES

$^{1}/_{2}$ pound mild Cheddar or American cheese, grated

$^{1}/_{2}$ cup mayonnaise

$^{1}/_{4}$ cup chopped sweet pickles

1 tablespoon seeded and grated red bell peppers

$^{1}/_{4}$ cup finely chopped green onions (green and white parts)

Dash of Tabasco brand pepper sauce

Combine all of the ingredients together and use immediately. Or, store in an airtight container for up to 1 week.

Olive and Pecan Cream Cheese Filling

MAKES ABOUT 2 CUPS, ENOUGH FOR ABOUT 80 FINGER SANDWICHES

Two 3-ounce packages cream cheese, at room temperature

¾ cup mayonnaise

½ cup chopped pecans

½ cup chopped green olives stuffed with pimentos

1 teaspoon brine juice from the olive jar

Dash of Tabasco brand pepper sauce

Combine all of the ingredients and mix well. Use immediately or store in an airtight container for as long as 1 week.

Several years ago, when Mr. Paul's daughter married here on the Island, he asked Eula Mae to think of something spectacular to fix for the wedding reception.

"I wasn't sure what I was going to do, but I had a few ideas running around inside my head," said Eula Mae with a wink.

But the problem, if there was one, was solved when Mr. Paul arrived one late afternoon with an ice chest filled with waterfowl—teals, mallards, geese.

"I cleaned them well and stored them in the freezer. When the wedding date drew near, I had everything I needed to make a wild game jambalaya. The guests at the reception went wild over this dish. The flavor of the game gave the jambalaya a real jolt!" Eula Mae recalled.

Be sure that you clean the waterfowl well, picking out the pin feathers, cleaning the cavities, and rinsing them thoroughly under cool water. It's also best to skin the birds, debone them, and cut the meat into small pieces before cooking.

WILD GAME JAMBALAYA

MAKES 20 TO 25 SERVINGS

Carcasses of 10 quail, 12 doves, 12 teals, and 4 geese
3 tablespoons vegetable oil
3 pounds game bird meat
1 tablespoon salt
1 teaspoon cayenne
1 teaspoon freshly ground black pepper
1 teaspoon Tabasco brand pepper sauce
3 cups chopped yellow onions
2 cups seeded and chopped green bell peppers
1½ cups chopped celery
4 garlic cloves, peeled
1 pound cubed boiled ham
1 pound smoked pork sausage, chopped
5 cups raw long-grain white rice
1 cup chopped green onions (green and white parts)
1 cup finely chopped fresh parsley leaves

1. Put the carcasses in a large stockpot (or two small ones) and add enough water to cover. Bring to a boil, then reduce the heat to medium-low and simmer for 2 hours. Remove from the heat and drain, reserving 8 cups of the broth.

2. Heat the oil in a large, heavy pot or Dutch oven over medium heat. Season the meat with the salt, cayenne, black pepper, and Tabasco. Add to the pot and brown well, stirring occasionally. Transfer the meat to a platter and set aside.

3. Add the onions, bell peppers, celery, and garlic and cook, stirring often, until lightly golden, about 10 minutes. Return the meat to the pot, add the ham and sausage, and cook, stirring, for 10 minutes. Add the broth and bring to a boil. Add the rice and stir to mix well. Reduce the heat to medium-low, cover, and cook until the rice is tender and the liquid has been absorbed, about 1 hour.

4. Add the green onions and parsley. Stir to mix well and adjust the seasonings, if necessary. Serve hot.

These miniature pecan pies, called tarts by Eula Mae, are fabulous. And indeed they should be. Eula Mae collects the pecans that fall to the ground in autumn all over the Island. She patiently cracks them and stores the meats in the freezer for later use.

She learned to make these tarts years ago and is quite proud of the flaky pastry dough that is made with cream cheese.

"If I had a nickel for every pecan tart I've made in the last fifty years, I would be very wealthy! Little children love them! But you should see the adults, they sneak into the kitchen during parties so they can have more without anyone seeing them!" says Eula Mae, laughing.

PARTY PECAN TARTS

MAKES 4 DOZEN

3 large eggs, lightly beaten

1 cup light corn syrup

1 cup sugar

2 tablespoons butter, melted

1 teaspoon pure vanilla extract

1 recipe Cream Cheese Pastry (page 54)

2½ cups finely chopped pecans

1. Combine the eggs, corn syrup, sugar, butter, and vanilla in a large mixing bowl and stir to mix well.

2. Preheat the oven to 350°F.

3. Remove the pastry from the refrigerator and spoon about 2 teaspoons of the chopped pecans into each pastry-lined muffin cup. Spoon about 2 teaspoons of the corn syrup mixture over the pecans in each muffin cup.

4. Bake until the corn syrup mixture sets and the tops of the tarts are lightly browned, 20 to 25 minutes. Remove from the oven and let cool in the pans for 5 minutes, then flip over onto a wire rack to cool another few minutes before serving. The tarts can be stored in an airtight container for up to a week.

Cream Cheese Pastry

MAKES 4 DOZEN PASTRIES

1 ¾ cups all-purpose flour

1 ½ teaspoons baking powder

⅛ teaspoon salt

¾ cup (1 ½ sticks) butter, at room temperature

Two 3-ounce packages cream cheese, at room temperature

1 ½ tablespoons sugar

1. Combine the flour, baking powder, and salt in a small mixing bowl and stir to mix.

2. Combine the butter, cream cheese, and sugar in a large mixing bowl and beat, using an electric mixer, on medium speed until smooth. Stir in the flour mixture and blend well. Press the dough firmly into 2 equal-size balls with your hands. Wrap the balls in plastic wrap and refrigerate for at least 1 hour.

3. Roll out the pastry, one ball at a time, to a ⅛-inch thickness on a lightly floured work surface with a lightly floured rolling pin. Cut into 2 ½-inch rounds. Press evenly into the bottoms and sides of forty-eight 1 ¾ x 1-inch muffin cups. Refrigerate for at least 1 hour before filling.

"**S**trawberries are always good to use for desserts. When I can, I use Louisi-ana strawberries, but they're only available in the spring. This is a grand cake, not individual smaller cakes, like you see in the stores. It's not really short-cake, but a regular rich butter cake," says Eula Mae. The clear vanilla flavoring called for here does not affect the color of the cream.

CELEBRATION STRAWBERRY SHORTCAKE

MAKES ONE 3-LAYER 9-INCH CAKE; SERVES 8 TO 10

$^1/_2$ cup (1 stick) plus 1 tablespoon butter, at room temperature

3 tablespoons granulated sugar

One 18$^1/_4$-ounce box yellow cake mix

3 large eggs

1 cup water

2 cups cold heavy cream

1 teaspoon clear vanilla flavoring

$^1/_3$ cup confectioners' sugar

2 pints fresh strawberries, hulled and sliced

1. Preheat the oven to 350°F. Butter three 9-inch cake pans with the 1 tablespoon butter. Sprinkle each evenly with the granulated sugar. Set aside.

2. Combine the cake mix, eggs, water, and remaining $^1/_2$ cup (1 stick) butter in a large mixing bowl. Stir to mix well, then beat, using an electric mixer, for 2 minutes.

3. Pour equal amounts of the cake batter into the prepared cake pans. Bake until golden brown, about 20 minutes. Remove from the oven and let cool in the pans for about 2 minutes. Turn out of the pans onto a wire rack to cool completely.

4. In a large cold stainless steel or glass bowl, combine the heavy cream, vanilla, and confectioners' sugar and beat, using an electric mixer, at high speed until soft peaks form.

5. Place one of the cake layers on a cake plate, spread about one third of the whipped cream on the top of the cake, and arrange one third of the strawberries over the cream. Top with the second layer and repeat the process. Top with the final layer and repeat the process. The cake can be served immediately or chilled.

SUMMER

"Summers can be unbearably hot in south Louisiana, *chère*.

When I was growing up, we didn't have air-conditioning, not

even electric fans. Taking care of our family garden, cooking on a

wood stove, and doing the chores

around the farm was hard, especially

in the summer. But even though we

were tired, we were happy. We

didn't know anything else. What is

that saying—ignorance is bliss? To

ward off the heat, we sometimes cooled a watermelon in the

water well. Ice, in a block, not crushed, was a luxury that

arrived only once a month, brought by a man from town in his

wagon. The ice was wrapped in sackcloth and stored in the

icebox. Yes, indeed, it was a box in which we stored the ice.

And we were very careful not to use ice unless necessary.

We chipped it with an ice pick and added the chips to cool our lemonade or water, but we used it sparingly," remembers Eula Mae.

But, although summertime brings hot and humid weather in south Louisiana, the amazing lushness of the Island offers a respite from the stifling, beating heat.

At early dawn, the stillness is broken only by the staccato "quock" of the stubby black-crowned night heron or the flapping wings of the great egrets or blue herons. A hazy mist floats above the cool waters of the marsh and bayous.

One might encounter a gregarious raccoon feeding on fish or a whiskered nutria plowing through a duckweed-covered pond. Alligators snooze in the quiet waters.

Delicate Spanish moss, shining with dew, sways gently in the morning breeze and there are splurges of riotous growth along the narrow roads that meander through the Island.

"And see there, *chère*, the tabasco peppers are growing, reaching for the sun, in the fields," says Eula Mae, as we ride slowly on the southeast side of the Island. "Let's check the summer gardens to see how the okra, tomatoes, eggplant, corn, and bell peppers are doing. We could make a gumbo with the okra and some shrimp. And we had best pick the tomatoes and eggplant before the sun gets too high."

Once the sun begins its journey overhead, the heat will set in, but a gentle wind from the Gulf of Mexico or a pop-up thunderstorm can often bring relief, if only briefly. A dip in Blue Hole, the Island's swimming spot, is a must on a hot summer afternoon.

"Oh, yes, we should make pitchers of homemade lemonade, or even spicy Bloody Marys for the guests. And perhaps bring them beer and soft drinks iced down in old metal tubs!" says Eula Mae, who is always thinking of ways to please.

Although it's hot and humid, many of the meals are enjoyed on the patios or in the yards in the shade of the giant oak trees.

Eula Mae tells me that it's nothing to make a large pot of gumbo or jambalaya for one of the families who might be visiting or staying at Marsh House. And there are always plenty of visitors during the summer who come to the Island to get away from the heat of the city.

"Listen, can you hear the whishing sounds of the bamboo in the late afternoon breeze? That's a favorite sound of mine here on the Island where there are many kinds of bamboo that were planted by Mr. Walter and his ancestors. Oh, and see the old oleanders with bright red, soft pink, and white flowers. Pretty, aren't they?"

When the shadows lengthen and deepen as dusk approaches, the Island takes on another personality.

The smells of the water-soaked marshes, honeysuckle, and verbena waft through the drowsy evening air as the comfortable chugging of boats coming in from the bay heralds the return of fishermen and shrimpers.

Trout and bream splash in the quiet bayous, the cypress and willow trees sway along the banks, and the sounds of cicadas, crickets, and toads rise and fall, filling the night as bedtime approaches.

Another summer day on the Island comes to an end.

AS I NOW DESCEND
INTO THE DARK
BOWELS OF THE EARTH,
I BESEECH THEE, SWEET
BARBARA, THAT I BE
KEPT SAFE FROM HARM,
FOR IT LIKETH ME NOT
THAT I RUSH UNBIDDEN
INTO GOD'S PRESENCE.

SUMMER BUFFET LUNCHEON

Avery Island Crabmeat Casserole

Artichoke and Crabmeat Salad

Vermilion Bay Crab Cakes

New Potatoes with Parsley

Garden Butter Beans

Charlotte Russe

It would seem almost too hot to cook during the summer, but not in south Louisiana. It's a way of life. Cooking and eating are entertainment.

During the summer, there are many gatherings either at Marsh House or at other homes on the Island. Family members who live elsewhere always flock to the Island when the weather gets warm. Some come for a week or so; others may stay longer. Whatever the reason for a get-together, the food is integral to the hospitality enjoyed on the Island.

Crabs, shrimp, and fresh summer produce from the garden are plentiful and ideal for lunches.

"The food is simple, but darling, oh, so good! Since there's usually a crowd that gathers to enjoy lunch, it's best to serve buffet style, so everyone can come back for second or more helpings. *Mais oui!*"

If there is a cool breeze, large tables are set up under the oak trees or on the wide porches of the old Island homes nestled in this subtropical wonderland, a perfect setting to enjoy a leisurely meal.

"This was a favorite of Sally Hewitt, the granddaughter of E. A. McIlhenny, who often served it for luncheons she held on the Island. She was very particular about this casserole and always stressed to me to have the finest crabmeat I could find. Of course, she was right. Only fresh lump crabmeat will make it special. One time, I ended up making ten casseroles for one of her famous gatherings and there wasn't a lick left!"

AVERY ISLAND CRABMEAT CASSEROLE

MAKES 6 TO 8 SERVINGS

1/2 cup (1 stick) butter

5 tablespoons all-purpose flour

1/2 pound white button mushrooms, wiped clean and thinly sliced

3 cups half-and-half

1/2 cup Sauterne wine

2 garlic cloves, peeled and smashed

Salt, cayenne, and white pepper to taste

2 pounds lump crabmeat, picked over for shells and cartilage

3/4 cup grated baby Swiss cheese

1/2 teaspoon sweet paprika

Toast points, crackers, or toasted croutons

1. Preheat the oven to 300°F.

2. Melt the butter in a large saucepan over medium heat. Add the flour and cook, stirring, until light blond, about 3 minutes. Add the mushrooms and coat well with the butter mixture. Add the half-and-half, wine, and garlic and season with salt, cayenne, and white pepper. Stir until smooth and thick. Gently fold in the crabmeat.

3. Pour the mixture into a buttered 9 x 13-inch dish and sprinkle evenly with the cheese and paprika. Bake until heated through and bubbly, about 25 minutes.

4. Serve hot with toast points or croutons for dipping.

"**S**ometimes salads need a little jolt! I've experimented over the years and tried adding things like cauliflower and colorful red, yellow, and green bell peppers, green beans, and radishes, all of which are available from the vegetable gardens on the Island."

When boiling anything green, like these fresh green beans, put a leaf of iceberg lettuce and a pinch of salt in the water to keep the color bright.

ARTICHOKE AND CRABMEAT SALAD

MAKES 8 SERVINGS

3 cups water

Pinch plus 1 teaspoon salt

1 cup fresh young green beans, ends trimmed

7 large leaves iceberg or Bibb lettuce leaves, rinsed and patted dry

Two 6-ounce jars quartered artichoke hearts packed in oil, drained

$1/4$ cup seeded and thinly sliced red bell peppers

$1/4$ cup seeded and thinly sliced green bell peppers

$1/2$ cup thinly sliced celery

$1/4$ cup sliced cauliflower

$1/4$ cup peeled, seeded, and cubed cucumbers

1 pound jumbo lump crabmeat, picked over for shells and cartilage

1 teaspoon Tabasco brand pepper sauce

$3/4$ cup Garlic Vinaigrette (recipe follows) or Thousand Island dressing

2 medium-size, ripe tomatoes, thinly sliced

2 large hard-boiled eggs, peeled and coarsely chopped

$1/4$ cup thinly sliced radishes

1. Put the water and a pinch of salt in a medium-size saucepan and bring to a boil. Add the beans and one lettuce leaf. Cook until the beans are tender, about 5 minutes. Remove from the heat, drain, and let cool.

2. Combine the beans, artichokes, bell peppers, celery, cauliflower, and cucumbers in a large salad bowl. Toss to mix. Add the crabmeat.

3. Combine the remaining 1 teaspoon salt, Tabasco, and dressing in a small mixing bowl and whisk to blend. Pour the mixture over the salad and gently toss so as not to break up the crabmeat. Cover the salad with plastic wrap and chill for at least 30 minutes or as long as 1 hour.

4. To serve, arrange a lettuce leaf on each of 6 salad plates. Put about 1 cup of the salad on the lettuce, then arrange a slice or two of tomato on top and scatter the top with equal portions of the chopped egg and radishes.

There are those who think a mixed green salad is mundane and boring. But if you have a good dressing, the salad will take on a great personality.

"I like to combine different kinds of lettuce, cherry tomatoes, and any kind of vegetables from the garden in my salads. I always say to use what is in season and don't be afraid to mix different vegetables together. Mr. Paul McIlhenny loves this vinaigrette on just about any kind of salad."

Garlic Vinaigrette

MAKES ABOUT 1 1/2 CUPS

2 large garlic cloves, peeled

1 teaspoon salt

2 tablespoons distilled white vinegar

White pepper or cracked black pepper to taste

1 teaspoon dry mustard

2 tablespoons mayonnaise

1 cup vegetable oil

1. Mash the garlic with the salt to form a paste. Add the vinegar and stir to blend with a fork. Pour into a small jar and add the pepper, mustard, mayonnaise, and vegetable oil. Tightly screw on the lid and shake the mixture well.

2. Store the dressing in the refrigerator for about 1 hour, then bring it to room temperature before serving. It will keep in the refrigerator for up to 1 week.

During the summer, when the crabs are plentiful in Vermilion Bay, these crab cakes are just the thing for a summer lunch. Everyone has his or her own version of crab cakes, sometimes called crab chops or crab patties in south Louisiana. Because of the large Catholic community in this area, they were often served on Fridays when meat was not allowed. Serve with Tartar Sauce (page 193).

VERMILION BAY CRAB CAKES

MAKES ABOUT 1 DOZEN

$^1/_2$ cup (1 stick) butter

$^1/_2$ cup seeded and chopped green bell peppers

$^1/_4$ cup seeded and chopped red bell peppers

$^1/_4$ cup seeded and chopped yellow bell peppers

1 cup finely chopped yellow onions

2 tablespoons all-purpose flour

$^1/_2$ cup milk

2 pounds lump crabmeat, picked over for shells and cartilage

1 large egg

$^1/_2$ teaspoon salt

$^1/_4$ teaspoon cayenne

$^1/_4$ teaspoon white pepper

2 tablespoons chopped fresh parsley leaves

1 tablespoon chopped green onions (green part only)

$1^1/_2$ cups Eula Mae's Homemade Bread Crumbs (white) (page 34)

Peanut oil for deep-frying

1. Melt the butter in a large skillet over medium heat. Add the bell peppers and yellow onions and cook, stirring, until soft, about 5 minutes. Add the flour and stir for 2 minutes. Add the milk and stir until the mixture is smooth and thick. Remove from the heat and let cool. When the mixture has cooled, fold in the crabmeat.

2. Lightly beat the egg with the salt, cayenne, and white pepper. Pour this over the crabmeat in a large mixing bowl and mix gently. Add the parsley and green onions and mix again. Divide the mixture into 12 equal portions and form into patties.

3. Dredge the patties in the bread crumbs on both sides and pat them gently.

4. Heat about 1 inch of the peanut oil in a large, heavy skillet. Fry two to three patties at a time until golden, about 2 minutes on each side. Drain on paper towels. Serve warm.

This may be a very simple dish, but when you have homegrown potatoes and fresh parsley from your garden, it can't be beat for taste. Even the most sophisticated diners come back for seconds.

"Be sure not to overcook the potatoes or they'll get mushy!" warns Eula Mae.

NEW POTATOES WITH PARSLEY

MAKES 4 SERVINGS

1 dozen new red potatoes
$1/4$ cup ($1/2$ stick) butter, melted
$1/4$ cup finely chopped fresh parsley leaves
$1/4$ teaspoon salt
$1/4$ teaspoon freshly ground black pepper
$1/8$ teaspoon white pepper

1. Put the potatoes in a large saucepan and cover with water. Bring to a boil over medium-high heat, then reduce the heat to medium. Cover and simmer until just fork tender, about 20 minutes. Drain.

2. Return the potatoes to the saucepan, add the butter, parsley, salt, black pepper, and white pepper, and toss gently to coat evenly. Serve immediately.

VARIATION Rather than toss the boiled potatoes with the butter and parsley, Eula Mae also likes to toss them with about $1/2$ cup thinly sliced red onions and a tablespoon or two of Garlic Vinaigrette (page 63). You can also substitute $1/4$ cup olive oil for the butter, add 2 tablespoons distilled white vinegar, and toss with the potatoes.

Butter beans, the ones that are as small as the nail on your little finger or a baby's earlobe, are the best in the world.

"I prefer these to the big ones that are as big as your ears! The baby limas grow well during the summer and I pick them just as soon as they peek out on the vines; that's when they are so sweet and tender. This recipe is quite a bit different from most. The egg yolk added at the end makes the dish creamy and so good, *oui*! Oh, and don't forget to let that garlic clove cook until it's very tender. If it doesn't 'melt,' give it a gentle push against the side of the pot."

GARDEN BUTTER BEANS

MAKES 4 TO 6 SERVINGS

1 tablespoon vegetable oil

1 cup chopped yellow onions

1 tablespoon chopped celery

$^1/_4$ cup seeded and chopped green bell peppers

$^1/_4$ cup seeded and chopped red bell peppers

$^1/_4$ cup seeded and chopped fresh tomatoes

1 pound baby limas, fresh or frozen

1 garlic clove, peeled

$1^1/_2$ cups water

1 teaspoon salt

2 teaspoons sugar

$^1/_4$ teaspoon Tabasco brand pepper sauce

$^1/_4$ teaspoon freshly ground black pepper

1 large egg yolk

1 teaspoon all-purpose flour

1. Heat the oil in a medium-size saucepan over medium heat. Add the onions and celery, and cook, stirring occasionally, until soft and lightly golden, about 5 minutes. Add the bell peppers and cook, stirring occasionally, for about 5 minutes. Add the tomatoes, limas, and garlic, cover, and cook for 30 minutes, stirring occasionally.

2. Add the water, cover, and simmer, stirring occasionally, for 30 minutes.

3. Add the salt, sugar, Tabasco, and black pepper, and stir to mix. Cover and simmer for 10 minutes.

4. Take the egg yolk and, with the tips of your fingers, grab the white nodule that is located around it, slip the pocket off, and let the yolk fall into a small bowl. Beat the yolk, then add the flour and beat again to blend. Add 1 tablespoon of the liquid from the bean pot and whisk to blend. Slowly add the mixture to the pot and stir. Cook for 1 minute, then remove from the heat and serve.

Charlotte russe, believed to have been created for the Russian Czar Alexander, is traditionally made with ladyfingers and pudding.

Eula Mae, wanting to make a special cake for a particular luncheon, did her homework. It has become so popular that she makes it often for luncheons and other family occasions.

"If you have to serve a crowd, the recipe can be doubled without any problem," says Eula Mae. "Since I can't always find those wonderful ladyfingers, I make a simple pound cake to line the bowl."

CHARLOTTE RUSSE

MAKES 8 TO 10 SERVINGS

2 cups milk

$1/2$ cup sugar

2 large eggs, lightly beaten

One $1/4$-ounce envelope gelatin dissolved in $1/4$ cup water

1 teaspoon pure almond or vanilla extract

1 cup heavy cream

1 recipe My Pound Cake (page 36)

$1/4$ cup sliced almonds (optional), toasted (see Note)

8 fresh mint leaves (optional)

1. Combine the milk, sugar, and eggs in the top of a double boiler set over simmering water. Cook, stirring constantly, until the mixture thickens slightly, about 10 minutes. Add the gelatin mixture and continue to cook, stirring, until smooth and thick and the mixture coats the back of a spoon. Stir in $1/2$ teaspoon of the extract. Remove from the heat and let cool completely.

2. Combine the heavy cream with the remaining $1/2$ teaspoon extract in a large mixing bowl and beat with an electric mixer until soft peaks form. Fold gently into the custard mixture.

3. Cut the pound cake into $1/4$-inch-thick slices and line the bottom and sides of a large glass bowl with them. Pour the custard mixture over the cake slices. If you want to make it festive, sprinkle the top with the toasted almonds or arrange mint leaves over the custard.

4. Cover and chill for at least 6 hours before serving.

5. To serve, scoop into small dessert bowls.

> **NOTE** To toast the almonds, preheat the oven to 300°F. Arrange the nuts evenly in a small shallow baking pan or cookie sheet. Toast until aromatic and lightly golden, 8 to 10 minutes.

FOURTH OF JULY BARBECUE

Country Lemonade

Pit-Barbecued Chicken

Barbecued Hamburgers for a Crowd

Eula Mae's Potato Salad

Commissary Cole Slaw

Rice Dressing

Homemade Vanilla Ice Cream

Summer Peach Cobbler

For years, everyone who worked and lived on the Island gathered for a Fourth of July celebration on the grounds near the old factory, where the corporate office now stands. Because MoNeg and Eula Mae ran the Commissary, they were in charge of getting the food together for a crowd that sometimes numbered three hundred or more.

"Of course, we had help from the other employees who lived on the Island," remembers Eula Mae.

Two of the men, Beb and Moon, made their barbecue sauce a day or so in advance so that the flavors could blend well before it was used on the chicken and hamburgers that were cooked during the day of the celebration.

Eula Mae explains their preparation: "MoNeg and I would season the chicken halves, sometimes as many as 350, the day before. We had a system. Put a layer of chickens in a large container, then sprinkle them with a seasoning mix made with salt and cayenne, then sprinkle them again with just the right amount of Tabasco!

Don't ask me how much! We just knew! The containers were tightly covered, then stored in the huge refrigerators at the Commissary for the night."

Early on the morning of the Fourth, pounds of potatoes and dozens of eggs were boiled for the potato salad. The custard for the homemade ice cream was already chilling, and the large fire pits were lit. All the men would be in charge of barbecuing the chicken and hamburgers.

"I can still see them, drinking a beer, talking around the smoking pits, and turning the chicken," Eula Mae recalls.

"Watermelons were kept iced down in big coolers and, later in the day, everyone took turns churning the ice cream! You can be assured that everyone went home tired but satisfied from the grand feast!"

"I can still see them, drinking a beer, talking around the smoking pits, and turning the chicken."

Don't ever let Eula Mae find you making lemonade from that powdered stuff you get at the supermarket.

"Lemons are cheap and the taste is so fresh and bright! You can garnish the lemonade with lemon wedges or slices, or a few sprigs of fresh mint from the garden."

Eula Mae suggests that you always keep a pitcher of lemonade chilling in the refrigerator during the hot months because it quenches thirst right away.

COUNTRY LEMONADE

MAKES ABOUT 8 SERVINGS

2 cups sugar

1 quart water

1 cup fresh lemon juice (from 8 to 10 lemons)

Lemon wedges or slices for garnish

Sprigs fresh mint for garnish

1. Combine the sugar and water in a large pitcher. Stir to dissolve the sugar. Add the lemon juice and stir to mix. Cover and chill in the refrigerator until ready to use.

2. To serve, add crushed ice to tall glasses and pour the lemonade over it. Garnish with lemon slices and mint.

Chicken should be cooked long and slow on a pit directly over a steady, low fire.

"We used pits made from fifty-gallon drums. Barbecuing takes a lot of attention and you have to be watchful for flare-ups. If the fire is too hot, the chicken will burn. You have to nurse the chickens while they cook. Standing around the barbecue pits was part of the event!"

You don't want to use butter in this recipe; it'll burn over the heat of the fire.

PIT-BARBECUED CHICKEN

MAKES 6 SERVINGS

1 tablespoon salt

2 teaspoons cayenne

1 teaspoon freshly ground black pepper

3 plump fryers (about 3 pounds each) cut in half

1 cup (2 sticks) margarine, melted, or 1 cup oil from Beb's Barbecue Sauce (page 74)

3 tablespoons Tabasco brand pepper sauce

1 cup Beb's Barbecue Sauce (page 74)

1. Combine the salt, cayenne, and black pepper in a small bowl and blend. Rub the chickens with the seasoning mix. Cover and chill for at least 2 hours.

2. Prepare a barbecue pit with a charcoal fire. The charcoal should be gray with ash and hot in the center. Melt the margarine (or heat the barbecue sauce oil) in a small saucepan and add the Tabasco. Put the chickens on the grill and baste frequently with the margarine or oil. Turn the chickens about every 20 minutes, but keep the lid closed in between basting and turning. The chickens will take about 2½ hours to cook.

3. Right before taking the chickens off the pit, brush liberally with the barbecue sauce.

"It takes a little work to make this sauce that Beb created, but I think you'll be more than happy with it. Make it a day or two in advance and store it in the refrigerator. We used to grind the vegetables in the kitchen at the Commissary because we had all the equipment, but you can do it with a hand grinder or in a food processor," explains Eula Mae.

After the sauce is made, you can skim off the oil that rises to the top and put it in a jar to use as a basting sauce while the chicken is cooking. This oil can also be used to baste hamburgers.

Just remember, this sauce is not used to baste the chicken during the long, slow cooking time, because it will burn. It's swabbed on the chicken or hamburgers when they're just about cooked. This sauce is also great to spoon over French bread. Cut the loaves in half lengthwise, then spread the sauce generously on the halves, wrap loosely in foil, set them on the pit, and let them get warm!

Beb's Barbecue Sauce

MAKES ABOUT 2 QUARTS

3 pounds yellow onions, cut into several large pieces

3 medium-size green bell peppers, seeded and cut into several large pieces

1 bunch celery, ends trimmed and cut into large lengths

Leaves from 1 bunch fresh parsley

1 bunch green onion tops

1 head garlic, separated into cloves and peeled

2 quarts vegetable oil

Three 8-ounce cans tomato sauce

Three 20-ounce bottles ketchup

One 10-ounce bottle Worcestershire sauce

3 tablespoons yellow mustard

3 tablespoons sugar

3 tablespoons salt

1 cup (2 sticks) butter

One 2-ounce bottle Tabasco brand pepper sauce

1. Place the yellow onions, bell peppers, celery, parsley, green onion tops, and garlic in a meat grinder or food processor and finely grind.

2. Combine the ground vegetables with the oil, tomato sauce, ketchup, Worcestershire, mustard, sugar, salt, butter, and Tabasco in a large, heavy pot and stir to mix. Cook, stirring often, over low heat for about 1½ hours.

3. Remove from the heat and let cool. Skim the oil that rises to the surface and reserve. Store the sauce and the oil in airtight containers for up to 2 days in the refrigerator or in the freezer for up to 3 months. Reheat it before you use it.

For the annual Fourth of July celebration on the Island, Eula Mae sometimes used twenty-five to fifty pounds of ground meats to make the hamburgers. The ladies would gather at the Commissary and mix the meat with the seasonings, then form the burgers into thick patties, which were then stored between layers of wax paper in the big refrigerators. This recipe makes a lot, but you can always cut it in half or more to accommodate your group.

"The burgers were supposed to be for the children, but the adults enjoyed them as well. You can use the oil from Beb's Barbecue Sauce to baste the burgers while they cook."

And don't forget to toast the buns right on the grill. They're so much better than warmed in the oven.

BARBECUED HAMBURGERS FOR A CROWD

MAKES ABOUT 32 PATTIES

6 pounds ground beef

2 pounds lean ground pork

1 cup finely chopped yellow onions

1½ tablespoons salt

1 tablespoon cayenne

1 tablespoon freshly ground black pepper

1 tablespoon Tabasco brand pepper sauce

2 tablespoons Worcestershire sauce

½ cup oil from Beb's Barbecue Sauce (page 74) or ½ cup vegetable oil

2 cups Beb's Barbecue Sauce (page 74)

1. Combine all the ingredients in a very large mixing bowl, except the oil and barbecue sauce, and mix well. Form into patties. Brush with the oil. Broil, fry, or grill to desired doneness. More oil can be brushed on the patties while they cook.

2. Right before taking the patties off the grill, brush them liberally with the barbecue sauce.

Eula Mae made me laugh one day when she told me she was going to show me how to make potato salad. I assured her that everyone made potato salad, although I did brag a bit on mine, which is made with lemony homemade mayonnaise.

"Perhaps that's your secret, but I also have mine. I like to add a bit of vinegar to the salad to give a little jolt!"

And, indeed, her potato salad is delicious. There are not too many gatherings on the Island where it isn't served. Eula Mae picks potatoes in the gardens on the Island when they are available, or chooses the best ones at the grocery store. The salad goes a long way when serving a crowd.

EULA MAE'S POTATO SALAD

MAKES ABOUT 16 SERVINGS

1 tablespoon salt

5 pounds medium-size red potatoes, peeled and quartered

1 dozen eggs

$^1/_2$ cup vegetable oil

1 teaspoon distilled white vinegar

2 cups Eula Mae's Homemade Mayonnaise (page 78)

$^1/_4$ teaspoon cayenne

1 teaspoon Tabasco brand pepper sauce

$^1/_4$ cup finely chopped sweet pickles

1 rib celery, chopped

$^1/_2$ medium-size green bell pepper, seeded and chopped

1. Fill a large, deep pot two thirds full with cold water and bring to a boil. Add the salt and potatoes. Cover and let cook over medium heat for 7 minutes, then carefully add the eggs. Continue to cook until the potatoes are fork tender, about 10 minutes.

2. Remove the eggs and drain the potatoes. Peel the eggs and separate the yolks from the whites. Mash the yolks in a large mixing bowl and stir in the oil and vinegar. Add the mayonnaise, cayenne, and Tabasco and stir to mix well.

3. Dice the potatoes and add to the mayonnaise mixture along with the pickles, celery, and bell pepper. Chop the egg whites and add to the salad. Stir to mix. Refrigerate for 15 minutes before serving.

"**I** often make my own mayonnaise, rather than buy it at the store. After all, the ingredients—vegetable oil, eggs, salt, vinegar—are usually at hand and I think the homemade has a different taste than the commercial kind. Long ago, before blenders and food processors, I did this by hand, adding a little oil at a time and blending it into the mixture with a fork. Nowadays, it's so much easier in a blender or processor. Oh, and since it has no preservatives, I recommend refrigerating the mayonnaise in an airtight container and using it within twenty-four hours."

Eula Mae's Homemade Mayonnaise

MAKES ABOUT 2 CUPS

2 large egg yolks, at room temperature

$1/4$ teaspoon dry mustard

$1/2$ teaspoon salt

$1/4$ teaspoon Tabasco brand pepper sauce

1 tablespoon distilled white vinegar

$1^3/4$ cups vegetable or olive oil

To make it by hand, combine the egg yolks, mustard, salt, Tabasco, and vinegar in a medium-size mixing bowl and whisk to blend well. Add the oil, about 2 tablespoons at a time, whisking in between each addition, until thick and smooth.

To make it in a blender or food processor, process the egg yolks for about 30 seconds. Add the mustard, salt, Tabasco, and vinegar. Pulse several times to blend. With the machine running, slowly drizzle in the oil through the feed tube until the mixture thickens.

Cole slaw is often served during the summer because it can be made ahead of time and chilled. And it goes with just about anything.

"Try dressing a sandwich with it. Years ago we dressed some of our sandwiches at the Commissary with this cole slaw and the customers loved it. Mr. Paul McIlhenny loves this, especially when I shave the cabbage. You can't get the same effect in a food processor. Take your time, and shave it with a sharp knife. It really makes a difference, *chère*."

COMMISSARY COLE SLAW

MAKE 6 SERVINGS

1 tablespoon distilled white vinegar

2 tablespoons mayonnaise

1 teaspoon sugar

$^1/_2$ teaspoon salt

$^1/_8$ teaspoon freshly ground black pepper

$^1/_2$ head white cabbage (about 1 pound), cored and shaved

4 baby carrots, finely grated

$^1/_2$ cup finely chopped red onions

$^1/_2$ cup chopped fresh tomatoes (optional)

1. Combine the vinegar, mayonnaise, sugar, salt, and black pepper in a jar fitted with a lid. Shake well and set aside.

2. Combine the cabbage, carrots, and onions in a large salad bowl. Add the dressing, toss to coat everything well, cover, and chill for at least 1 hour and up to a day before serving.

3. If you wish, scatter the tomatoes over the slaw when serving.

"**R**ice dressing is standard fare at barbecues, but is also included on the menu for holiday meals and Sunday dinners. Sometimes visitors call it dirty rice because the browned meats and the roux that are mixed with the rice are rather brown, like dirt! But we don't ever call it dirty rice. That doesn't sound very nice. Rice dressing sounds so much better, *non*?"

Eula Mae advises not to add the liver until the end of the cooking time.

"It gets tough and bitter, and that's not good."

RICE DRESSING

MAKES 8 TO 10 SERVINGS

$1/4$ cup peanut oil

$1/4$ cup all-purpose flour

2 pounds ground beef chuck

1 pound ground pork shoulder

1 pound chicken gizzards, cleaned and ground

1 tablespoon salt

1 teaspoon Tabasco brand pepper sauce

1 teaspoon freshly ground black pepper

2 cups chopped yellow onions

1 cup seeded and chopped green bell peppers

1 cup chopped celery

3 garlic cloves, peeled

$1/2$ cup chopped fresh parsley leaves

$1/2$ cup chopped green onions (green and white parts)

$1/2$ pound chicken livers, cleaned and ground

2 cups raw long-grain white rice, cooked according to package instructions

1. Heat the oil for 2 minutes in a large, heavy saucepan over medium heat. Add the flour and, stirring constantly and slowly, make a roux the color of chocolate (see Eula Mae's advice on making a roux, page 94). Add the ground beef, pork, and chicken gizzards and season with the salt, Tabasco, and black pepper. Reduce the heat to medium-low and cook, covered, stirring occasionally, for 30 minutes.

2. Add the yellow onions, bell peppers, celery, and garlic, cover, and cook, stirring occasionally, until the mixture thickens, about 1 hour.

3. Add the parsley, green onions, and chicken liver. Cook, stirring occasionally, until all the pink in the liver disappears, about 10 minutes. Add the cooked rice and stir to blend well and heat through. Remove from the heat and serve warm.

"We call this *crème à la glace* in south Louisiana. It's a thick, rich custard that becomes the best ice cream once it's churned in an ice cream machine. Of course, I always made it in one of those hand-cranked contraptions. Part of the fun was huddling around, having some of the children take turns turning the crank, then, when it got harder to turn, the men and women took over. Then we wrapped the machine in burlap sacks and packed ice and rock salt to let the ice cream 'cure' while it firmed up."

Any fresh fruit, like berries or peaches, can be added to the mixture before you churn. Berries can be left whole. Stone fruit should be peeled, pitted, and coarsely chopped, and bananas should be peeled and coarsely chopped.

HOMEMADE VANILLA ICE CREAM

MAKES ABOUT 2 QUARTS

8 large eggs

2 cups sugar

One 14-ounce can sweetened condensed milk

One 12-ounce can evaporated milk

2 tablespoons all-purpose flour

2 tablespoons cornstarch

1 quart whole milk

1 quart half-and-half

1 tablespoon pure vanilla extract

1. Beat the eggs well in a large mixing bowl. Slowly add the sugar and continue to beat until well blended. Add the condensed milk, evaporated milk, flour, cornstarch, and milk and stir to blend well. Pour the mixture into a large, heavy pot over medium-low heat. Stir constantly until the mixture thickens enough to coat the back of a spoon, 30 to 45 minutes.

2. Stir in the half-and-half and vanilla. Remove from the heat and let cool. Cover and refrigerate for at least 2 hours.

3. Pour the mixture into the ice cream maker and process according to the manufacturer's directions.

"**D**uring the heat of the summer, the peaches grown in Ruston, Louisiana, in the northern part of the state, are at their peak. They are so good that my daughter and I get as many as possible. One year, we ordered about forty-two crates that we shared with some of our friends. We put most in the freezer for later use, but we also make a cobbler that I think is delicious."

SUMMER PEACH COBBLER

MAKES 8 TO 10 SERVINGS

CRUST

1 cup all-purpose flour

$\frac{1}{4}$ teaspoon salt

$\frac{1}{2}$ cup (1 stick) cold butter, cut into pieces, plus 1 tablespoon butter, at room temperature

3 to 4 tablespoons ice water, as needed

PEACHES

7 to 8 ripe peaches

5 tablespoons sugar

$\frac{1}{2}$ cup (1 stick) butter

2 tablespoons cornstarch

$\frac{1}{2}$ cup water

1. To make the crust, sift the flour and salt into a large mixing bowl. Add the cold butter and work it in with your fingertips until it resembles coarse meal. Add the cold water, a tablespoon at a time, mixing until the dough comes together to form a smooth ball. Wrap in plastic wrap and chill for about 30 minutes.

2. Butter an 8 x 12-inch baking dish with the softened butter. Set aside.

3. Bring a pot of water to a rolling boil. Drop the peaches into the boiling water and boil until the skin begins to loosen from the flesh, 30 seconds to 1 minute. Quickly transfer the peaches to a colander and let cool a bit. Gently remove the skins. Cut the peaches in half horizontally, and remove the pits. Slice crosswise into ½-inch pieces.

4. Put the peach slices in a large skillet over low heat. Sprinkle with 3 tablespoons of the sugar. When the peaches begin to throw off some of their juices, add the butter and melt completely, stirring gently so as not to break up the peaches. Combine the remaining 2 tablespoons sugar, the cornstarch, and water in a measuring cup and whisk to blend, dissolving the sugar and cornstarch. Add the mixture to the skillet and stir gently until the liquid becomes clear and thick. Remove from the heat. Pour the mixture into the prepared baking dish and let cool slightly.

5. Preheat the oven to 350°F.

6. Meanwhile, take the dough out of the refrigerator and roll it out on a lightly floured work surface to about ¼ inch thick. With a sharp knife, cut long strips about ½ inch wide. Arrange the strips over the peaches in the baking dish in a lattice pattern.

7. Bake until the crust is lightly browned, about 30 minutes. Remove from the oven and let cool slightly before serving.

FAIS DO-DO

Seafood Gumbo

Crab and Shrimp Étouffée

Walter Doré's Crab and Shrimp Sauce Piquante

Eula Mae's Crab and Shrimp Sauce Piquante

Red (or White) Beans, Eula Mae's Way

Maque Choux

Pineapple Upside-Down Cake, My Way

Blackberry Patch Cobbler

A *fais do-do* (FAY-DOE-DOE) means to "go to sleep" or "sleep." But, in reality, it's like a Cajun hoedown, a country dance. Because there were few public dance halls, families often gathered on Saturdays, bringing all the children, even very young babies, to enjoy eating as well as dancing. The music, sometimes referred to by the locals as "chanky-chank," was provided by an accordion, a fiddle, and a "ting-a-ling," or triangle. The favored dance of the Cajuns is called a two-step and is akin to a waltz, but livened up with little jig steps.

"*Mais oui*," says Eula Mae, "we sometimes danced until dawn. And sometimes, we danced outside under the trees because the houses were rather small. *La poussière*—the dust—would fly under our feet!"

Babies were often put to sleep in another room with a grandmother or other older family member to keep them quiet while the band played on. But sometimes, a mother would hold her baby in her lap until she got up to dance, handing her child to someone else.

Oh, yes, a *fais do-do* was a good time—a good time for everyone to catch up on the news, see cousins and other relatives, and, of course, eat! More often than not, everyone brought a dish. One family might bring a gumbo or stew; another supplied seafood to boil or fish to fry, and there were always sweet treats, like cakes, cookies, or some kind of dessert made with local fruits.

—a good time for everyone

to catch up on the news, see

cousins and other relatives,

and, of course, eat!

Gumbo, made with the ubiquitous roux, is probably the best-known dish to come out of south Louisiana. Gumbo is a hearty, thick stew, made so by the addition of a roux, which is nothing more than flour and oil, slowly stirred over heat until it reaches the color of peanut butter or chocolate, depending on what kind of gumbo you're preparing. For instance, a lighter roux is preferred for a seafood gumbo so as not to overpower the delicate meat. On the other hand, a darker roux is favored for chicken and sausage, duck, and rabbit.

When the Acadians arrived in south Louisiana, they found a variety of seafood and wild game. Being quite resourceful, they realized they could make a meal in one pot. You will find gumbos made with just about anything—chicken and sausage, shrimp, crab, and oysters, ducks, squirrels, and rabbits. Eula Mae favors seafood gumbo when fresh shrimp and crabs are available.

And you should know that gumbo is an African word. It has long been thought to be French, but gumbo is really a Portuguese corruption of *quin gombo*, which in turn is a corruption of *guillobo*, the native word for okra in the Congo and Angola area of Africa. It is believed that the slaves shipped to America carried okra seeds in their hair because they wanted to bring something of home with them. The seeds were planted and, *voilà*, okra for making gumbo!

"Now don't forget, you can't rush the cooking process. Cook it slowly and you'll be rewarded with a delicious meal. Serve it in bowls with cooked long-grain rice," Eula Mae reminds us.

SEAFOOD GUMBO

MAKES 6 TO 8 SERVINGS

5 tablespoons vegetable oil

1 pound medium-size fresh okra, trimmed and cut into $1/4$-inch-thick rounds, or one 16-ounce package frozen sliced okra, thawed

4 teaspoons distilled white vinegar

1 cup all-purpose flour

$1^{1}/_{4}$ cups chopped yellow onions

$1^{1}/_{4}$ cups chopped green onions (green and white parts)

1 garlic clove, minced

2 cups seeded and chopped green bell peppers

1 cup chopped celery

2 tablespoons chopped fresh parsley leaves

Two 16-ounce cans whole tomatoes, with their liquid, chopped

1 cup cubed boiled ham

2 cups shrimp stock (see page 89) or water

2 bay leaves

2 sprigs fresh thyme

1 tablespoon Worcestershire sauce

1 teaspoon Tabasco brand pepper sauce

1 teaspoon salt

1 pound medium-size shrimp, peeled and deveined

1 pound lump crabmeat, picked over for shells and cartilage

Hot cooked long-grain white rice (see page 171)

1. Heat 3 tablespoons of the oil in a medium-size skillet (not a cast-iron skillet, because it will cause the okra to discolor) over medium heat. Add the okra and cook, stirring frequently, for about 30 minutes. Add the vinegar and cook until the okra is no longer ropey or slimy and is lightly browned, about 10 minutes. Remove from the heat and set aside.

2. In a large, heavy pot or Dutch oven, heat the remaining 2 tablespoons oil over medium heat for 2 minutes and add the flour. Cook, stirring slowly and constantly, to make a dark brown roux (see Eula Mae's advice on making a roux, page 94). Add the yellow onions, 1 cup of the green onions, the garlic, bell peppers, celery, and 1 tablespoon of the parsley and cook, stirring often, until the vegetables are tender and lightly golden, about 10 minutes. Add the tomatoes, ham, okra, shrimp stock, bay leaves, thyme, Worcestershire, Tabasco, and salt. Reduce the heat to medium-low and simmer, covered, for 45 minutes.

3. Add the shrimp and crabmeat and simmer until the shrimp turn pink, 8 to 10 minutes. Remove and discard the bay leaves and thyme. Garnish with the remaining ¼ cup green onions and 1 tablespoon parsley.

4. Serve the gumbo over rice and pass additional Tabasco at the table.

É*touffer* simply means "to smother." Crawfish *étouffée* is the most popular, but *étouffées* can be made with any kind of seafood, as well as chicken, turtle, or rabbit. Traditional *étouffée* does not have a roux, but most have some kind of thickener. The reason we're using butter and flour here is to give the dish some substance and body to make the gravy a little thick and very smooth.

"I always check my crabmeat before leaving the place of purchase. You want the very best and I know the best places around here, so I always give them my business. But then, when I get it home, I check again, and go through it delicately to remove anything that looks unattractive," says Eula Mae.

CRAB AND SHRIMP ÉTOUFFÉE

MAKES 8 TO 10 SERVINGS

$^{1}/_{2}$ cup (1 stick) butter

$^{1}/_{3}$ cup all-purpose flour

2 cups chopped yellow onions

1 rib celery, chopped

2 large garlic cloves, peeled

$^{1}/_{3}$ cup seeded and chopped red bell peppers

$^{1}/_{3}$ cup seeded and chopped green bell peppers

1 cup water

2 pounds medium-size shrimp, peeled and deveined

$1^{1}/_{4}$ teaspoons salt

1 teaspoon Tabasco brand garlic pepper sauce

$^{1}/_{2}$ teaspoon freshly ground black pepper

$^{1}/_{4}$ cup chopped green onions (green and white parts)

$^{1}/_{4}$ cup chopped fresh parsley leaves

2 pounds jumbo lump crabmeat, picked over for shells and cartilage

Hot cooked long-grain white rice (see page 171)

1. In a large, heavy pot, over medium-low heat, melt the butter, then add the flour. Stirring often, cook until the foam subsides and the mixture turns a golden color, like sandpaper, 10 to 12 minutes (see page 94 for Eula Mae's advice on making a roux). Add the yellow onions, celery, and garlic. Cook, stirring often, until soft and golden, about 15 minutes.

2. Add the bell peppers and cook, stirring occasionally, for 5 minutes. Add the water and stir to blend until the mixture thickens. Add the shrimp and stir to mix. Cook, stirring occasionally, until the shrimp turn pink, 5 to 7 minutes. Add the salt, Tabasco, and black pepper and continue to cook for 5 to 7 minutes longer. Add the green onions, parsley, and crabmeat. Don't stir or you'll break up the crabmeat. Gently shake the pot, cover, and simmer for 5 minutes. Turn off the heat and let it rest (with the lid on the pot) for about 5 minutes.

3. Serve over the rice in soup or gumbo bowls.

Making Shrimp Stock

Making shrimp stock is quite easy. If you are able to get fresh shrimp with their heads and shells on, do so. Simply break off the heads and peel the shrimp. Put the heads and peelings in a large pot and fill with enough water to cover them. You can add the peelings of yellow onions (to give the stock a wonderful golden color) as well as a rib or two of celery (coarsely chopped). Bring to a boil, then reduce the heat to medium-low and simmer, uncovered, for about 1 hour. Strain in a colander or sieve and there you have it. The stock can be stored in an airtight container (or in several small ones) in the freezer for up to 3 months.

This is one of those one-pot dishes that is so popular for get-togethers in south Louisiana.

"MoNeg loved to cook. After we added a bigger kitchen back of the Commissary, he experimented with all sorts of dishes. Mr. Walter would often stop by to see what MoNeg was cooking, and he was regularly asked to cook a meal for Mr. Walter's dinner parties. When MoNeg prepared this dish, he claimed that it 'made your tongue go crazy.' He allowed one crab per person, but the recipe may serve more than fifteen. We both loved to cook and he especially enjoyed spending hours in the kitchen making this dish for the McIlhennys when they had guests on the Island."

WALTER DORÉ'S CRAB AND SHRIMP SAUCE PIQUANTE

MAKES ABOUT 15 SERVINGS

15 large live blue crabs

1 cup vegetable oil

³/₄ cup all-purpose flour

6 medium-size ripe tomatoes, coarsely chopped

1 teaspoon sugar

3¹/₂ cups chopped yellow onions

2 cups seeded and chopped green bell peppers

3 ribs celery, chopped

4 garlic cloves, minced

Three 12-ounce cans tomato paste

One 8-ounce can tomato sauce

One 10-ounce can tomatoes and green chiles, with its liquid

2 cups water

1 teaspoon Tabasco brand pepper sauce

¹/₂ teaspoon cayenne

4 bay leaves

Salt and freshly ground black pepper to taste

5 pounds jumbo shrimp, peeled and deveined

Hot cooked long-grain white rice (see page 171)

1. Wash the crabs under cold running water to remove all the sand. Using long-handled tongs, drop them, several at a time, into a large pot of boiling water. Cover and cook until the shells are bright red, 5 to 10 minutes. Remove the crabs with the tongs and set aside to cool. Repeat with the remaining crabs.

2. Break off the crab claws, crack, and set aside. Place each crab on its back. Remove and discard the small piece at the lower part of the shell that terminates in a point (the apron). Remove the fat beneath the apron and set aside. Holding the crab in both hands, insert your thumb or a blunt knife under the shell by the apron hinge. Remove and discard the top shell. Remove the spongy substance (the gills) that lies under the tapering points on either side of the crab back. Set the crab body aside.

3. Combine the oil and flour in a large, heavy pot or Dutch oven and cook over medium-low heat, stirring constantly, until the roux is the color of peanut butter, about 30 minutes (see Eula Mae's advice on making a roux, page 94).

4. Add the tomatoes, sugar, onions, bell peppers, celery, and garlic, stirring to mix. Cook, stirring often, until the vegetables are soft, about 5 minutes. Add the tomato paste, tomato sauce, tomatoes and chiles, and water. Simmer, uncovered, for 10 minutes, stirring frequently. Add the crab fat, Tabasco, cayenne, bay leaves, salt, and black pepper. Cover and simmer for 2 to 2½ hours, stirring occasionally; it'll be thick like a stew.

5. Add the crab claws, cover, and simmer for 5 minutes. Add the crabs, cover, and simmer an additional 10 minutes. Stir in the shrimp, cover, and simmer for 30 minutes, stirring occasionally.

6. Remove from the heat, uncover, and let stand for 10 minutes. Serve over the rice.

The Cajun sauce *piquante*, not to be confused with picante sauce (the Mexican peppery mixture used for dipping), is a much-loved south Louisiana dish that is indeed spicy and peppery, but more like a stew. It is made with a roux, tomatoes, and, of course, onions, bell peppers, celery, garlic, and whatever is available—seafood, fowl, game, and other local meats. There are many different variations.

"MoNeg had his own recipe and I have mine. This one is a little easier to eat because the crabmeat is out of the shell. It's very rich and filling and is another one of those Acadian one-pot dishes."

It is usually served in deep bowls over white long-grain rice.

EULA MAE'S CRAB AND SHRIMP SAUCE PIQUANTE

MAKES 8 TO 10 SERVINGS

1 cup peanut oil

¾ cup all-purpose flour

3½ cups chopped yellow onions

1 cup chopped celery

6 garlic cloves, peeled

1 cup seeded and chopped green bell peppers

1 cup seeded and chopped red bell peppers

One 6-ounce can tomato paste

One 8-ounce can tomato sauce

One 10-ounce can diced tomatoes with green chiles

Salt and freshly ground black pepper to taste

¾ teaspoon Tabasco brand pepper sauce

4 bay leaves

2 pounds medium-size shrimp, peeled and deveined

2 pounds jumbo lump crabmeat, picked over for shells and cartilage

1 cup water, or more as needed

2 tablespoons chopped fresh flat-leaf parsley leaves

1. Heat the oil in a large, heavy pot or Dutch oven over medium heat for 2 minutes. Add the flour and, stirring slowly and constantly, make a roux the color of peanut butter (see page 94). It will take 20 to 30 minutes.

2. Add the onions, celery, and garlic and cook, stirring, until soft, about 8 minutes. Add the bell peppers and cook, stirring, for 3 minutes. Add the tomato paste, tomato sauce, and tomatoes with chiles and stir to mix well. Season with salt, black pepper, and $\frac{1}{4}$ teaspoon of the Tabasco. Add the bay leaves. Reduce the heat to medium-low, cover the pot, and let simmer for 1 hour.

3. Sprinkle $\frac{1}{4}$ teaspoon of the Tabasco on the shrimp and the remaining $\frac{1}{4}$ teaspoon Tabasco on the crabmeat. Add the shrimp to the tomato sauce and cook, stirring gently once or twice, until they turn pink, about 6 minutes.

4. Add the water and cook, stirring occasionally, for 5 minutes. (The sauce should be thick and smooth. If it appears to be too dry, add a little more water.) Gently fold in the crabmeat. Do not stir; gently shake the pot. Cover and cook for 10 minutes. Remove the bay leaves, add the parsley, and serve hot over the rice.

How to Make a Roux

There are really no hard and fast rules about making a roux in south Louisiana. Every cook has his or her own method. Some will tell you that a roux is made by combining equal parts of oil (usually vegetable oil, though, in the old days, lard was used) and all-purpose flour in a cold, heavy pot and stirring it slowly and constantly over medium heat until the desired color is reached. Then again, some cooks choose to heat the oil a bit before adding the flour and continuing with the cooking. And yet others may prefer heating the pot before adding the oil-flour mixture all at once. There is also debate about the ratio of oil to flour. Some like more oil; others prefer more flour.

It really doesn't matter how it is made. What does matter is that, should it burn, it's best to throw it out and begin again. A burnt roux will make whatever dish you are preparing taste awful.

The roux that is made in south Louisiana is the base for many of the local dishes, such as gumbo, stews, and some gravies. The color of the roux can range from blond to medium to dark, depending on what type of dish you are preparing. For example, a crab stew may be made with a blond roux, while a dark roux is used for most gumbos.

Here is Eula Mae's technique:

"I usually prefer peanut oil because it doesn't have an odor and it doesn't smoke. But corn oil is also acceptable. Some cooks like vegetable oil, and that's okay too. Everyone has his or her preference. I like a little less oil than flour because I like a thick roux. I like to use a cast-iron pot, but if you don't have that, any heavy pot that heats evenly is fine. The amount of time it takes to cook your roux will depend on the type of pot. I like to cook my roux over a medium heat. And once you get it going, it shouldn't be left unattended. You don't want to burn it because you'll have to start all over again."

$^3/_4$ cup peanut oil

1 cup all-purpose flour

Heat the oil in a heavy (preferably cast-iron) pot over medium heat for about 2 minutes. Add the flour and blend. Stir slowly and constantly. To make a blond roux, the color of sandpaper, it will take about 8 minutes. For a roux the color of peanut butter, cook for about 12 minutes. A dark roux, one the color of chocolate, will take 15 to 18 minutes. As it cooks, the roux will thicken.

Eula Mae always says to make the roux a little darker than you want it because once the vegetables, broth, or water are added, it will lighten up just a bit.

"**W**e ate more white beans than red beans. Red beans is a New Orleans thing. But any kind is good to serve anytime. Sometimes if I have a ham bone, I put that in the pot as well. This makes a lot, so you can cut the recipe in half, or freeze the beans for later use."

RED (OR WHITE) BEANS, EULA MAE'S WAY

MAKES ABOUT 20 SERVINGS

$1/4$ cup bacon drippings

$3^1/2$ cups chopped yellow onions

2 cups seeded and chopped green bell peppers

$1^1/2$ cups chopped celery

3 garlic cloves, peeled

1 pound salt pork, cut into small chunks

2 pounds dried red kidney beans or 1 pound navy beans, picked over and rinsed in cool water

2 teaspoons salt

$1/4$ teaspoon freshly ground black pepper

$1/4$ teaspoon Tabasco brand pepper sauce

4 bay leaves

Chopped green onions for garnish

Chopped fresh parsley leaves for garnish

Hot cooked long-grain white rice (see page 171)

1. Heat the bacon drippings in a large, heavy pot or Dutch oven over medium heat. Add the onions, bell peppers, and celery and cook, stirring, until lightly golden, about 10 minutes. Add the garlic and salt pork and cook for 5 minutes. Add the beans and enough water to cover. Stir in the salt, black pepper, Tabasco, and bay leaves, bring to a boil, then reduce the heat to medium-low. Cook, partially covered, until the beans are tender and the mixture is creamy, about 2 hours, stirring occasionally. Add more water or broth if the mixture becomes dry.

2. Remove and discard the bay leaves. Serve hot, garnished with green onions and parsley, over rice.

There really is no literal translation for *maque choux*. This dish is made with corn, and the French word for corn is *maïs*. *Choux* is French for cabbage, but there's no cabbage in this favorite Acadian summer dish. Just know that it tastes very good!

"*Mon amie*, don't worry about the words, just enjoy it. It goes well with just about anything, from fried chicken or fish to stews and sauce piquantes. When you can, pick the corn yourself, or get it as fresh as possible from your vegetable stand. After picking the corn, I husk and clean it well and scrape the corn off the cobs immediately. The 'milk' from the cobs is what makes this dish so good! To extract the milk, I cut the top of the kernels with the tip of a sharp knife, then shave off the corn and scrape the cobs well. Sure, it takes time, but remember, you have to have that TLC!"

MAQUE CHOUX

MAKES ABOUT 4 SERVINGS

2 tablespoons butter

$1/2$ cup chopped yellow onions

$1/2$ cup seeded and chopped green bell peppers

4 cups corn kernels (canned, fresh, or frozen, thawed)

1 medium-size ripe tomato, peeled and chopped

$1/4$ teaspoon salt

$1/2$ teaspoon Tabasco brand pepper sauce

1. Melt the butter in a large, heavy saucepan over medium heat. Add the onions and bell peppers and cook, stirring often, until soft, about 5 minutes.

2. Add the corn, tomato, salt, and Tabasco. Reduce the heat to medium-low and simmer, uncovered, until the corn is tender, 10 to 15 minutes. Serve hot.

"Some people may think pineapple upside-down cake is rather *passé* and ordinary. But, you know, it's almost impossible to find a recipe for this simple old-fashioned cake in current cookbooks. I make mine in a Bundt cake pan and I think you'll find it a little different than most upside-down cakes. If you want to dress it up, serve it with a scoop of ice cream or some whipped cream."

PINEAPPLE UPSIDE-DOWN CAKE, MY WAY

MAKES 1 CAKE; SERVES 10 TO 12

$1/4$ cup ($1/2$ stick) butter, at room temperature, cut into thin slices

1 cup firmly packed dark brown sugar

One 20-ounce can pineapple chunks, drained, 1 cup of the juice reserved

24 maraschino cherries

One $18^{1}/4$-ounce box moist deluxe yellow cake mix

3 large eggs

$1/4$ cup peanut oil

1. Preheat the oven to 350°F.

2. Smear the butter onto the sides and bottom of a Bundt pan ("use your hands; nothing works better than those natural tools"). Then press the brown sugar evenly over the butter. Press the pineapple chunks into the wide section of the inside of the Bundt pan, on the bottom and sides, 3 to 5 chunks per section. Fill in with cherries (about 3) in a line in between the pineapple sections and press down gently. Set aside.

3. Put the cake mix in a large mixing bowl and make a well in the center. Add the eggs, the reserved pineapple juice, and peanut oil in the well. Beat with an electric mixer on medium speed until well blended and smooth, scraping down the bowl with a rubber spatula, about 2 minutes. Pour the batter into the prepared pan and spread the top evenly.

4. Bake until golden and the top springs back when touched lightly with your fingers, 45 to 50 minutes. Immediately place a platter over the top of the pan and turn it over, but do not remove the cake pan. Let stand for about 2 minutes, then remove the pan. You can serve warm, or let cool to room temperature.

"I wish all children could have the opportunity to pick blackberries! It's such a wonderful way to spend some time outdoors. I still love to go searching for the plump berries along the fence lines and footpaths, enjoying the quiet and peace, whistling a little tune, and poking through the brambles. Sometimes my arms get scratched and I might see a snake or two, but I just think of the good things we can make with our berries."

A traditional cobbler is a dessert made with fruit over which a biscuit crust is layered, then baked. Eula Mae changes her cobbler a bit by adding drop biscuits on top of the fruit.

"*Chère*, when you want to freeze blackberries, here's the best way. Do not rinse the berries with water. Simply pack them loosely in plastic freezer bags. When ready to use, defrost, then rinse them in cool water and drain well."

This recipe makes enough to serve about twenty, but you can certainly cut the recipe in half.

BLACKBERRY PATCH COBBLER

MAKES ABOUT 20 SMALL SERVINGS

1 gallon fresh blackberries, picked over

$3^1/_2$ cups sugar

2 tablespoons cornstarch

$3/_4$ cup ($1^1/_2$ sticks) butter, at room temperature

4 large eggs

1 teaspoon pure vanilla extract

$2^1/_2$ cups cake flour

2 teaspoons baking powder

$1/_4$ teaspoon salt

$1/_4$ cup water

Vanilla ice cream (optional)

1. Preheat the oven to 350°F.

2. Combine the berries and 2 cups of the sugar in a large, deep pot over medium heat. Cook, stirring occasionally, until a syrup forms, about 10 minutes. Remove $1/_2$ cup of the hot berry

juice and dissolve the cornstarch in it. Return this to the berry mixture and stir until the mixture thickens, then remove from the heat.

3. Combine ½ cup (1 stick) of the butter, the remaining 1½ cups sugar, and the eggs in a large mixing bowl and mix until smooth. Add the vanilla and stir to blend.

4. Sift the cake flour, baking powder, and salt into another large mixing bowl. Add the butter mixture and water. Stir to blend.

5. Smear the remaining 4 tablespoons (½ stick) butter over the bottom of an 18 x 12 x 2-inch baking dish. Pour the berry mixture into the dish. Spoon the batter, about 2 tablespoons at a time, to form drop biscuits or dumplings over the top of the berry mixture. Bake until the dough is golden and the mixture bubbles, 55 minutes to 1 hour.

6. Scoop a large spoonful of the berries with a biscuit into each dessert bowl. Serve with the ice cream, if you wish.

AUGUST FISHING TRIP

Corn Off the Cob Soup

Eula Mae's Chicken and Ham Jambalaya

Dried Shrimp and Egg Gumbo

Ti Gâteau Sec

South Louisiana Lemon Pie

When Mr. Walter S. McIlhenny was alive, he had a grand boat called *The Heron*, which he bought after he got out of the Marine Corps. It was originally built as an air-sea rescue boat for wartime service in the Mediterranean. Mr. Walter converted it into a pleasure/fishing boat that he often took out for weekends in the waters of the nearby Gulf of Mexico. His friends, whom he loved to entertain, often accompanied him.

"Oh, my, I remember them heading out on Fridays with Ti Bruce Broussard, who cooked onboard," recalls Eula Mae.

"Ti Bruce could tell you about those outings, when he would cook turtle soup, boiled shrimp, and fried fish. I can remember that Mr. Walter loved taking young children on the big boat, and making ice cream on board. And, of course, there was the time he caught a 150-pound tarpon and naturally he was quite excited."

It's been told too that on a holiday, Mr. Walter might take some of the men from the plant on a fishing trip, during which he would serve them a meal of gumbo or chicken stew and would insist on cleaning up after the meal.

The boat and Mr. Walter are gone, but the younger people have boats of their own and, be assured, they enjoy lots of food on their outings on the water.

When they catch fish, there's a fish supper. If they have fresh shrimp, they might boil some. But sometimes they bring prepared food on board, just in case they don't have any luck!

The younger people have boats of their own and, be assured, they enjoy lots of food on their outings on the water.

"I like to make corn soup when it's in season during the summer months. And, of course, there are all kinds of fresh garden vegetables in the summer, like tomatoes, to add to the soup. But I always put up fresh corn in the freezer because it's so simple to do. Simply cut the corn off the cobs, scraping to release the milk on the cob. Put the corn in a plastic storage bag and freeze. And if you put up, freeze, or can vegetables, you'll have them around in your pantry. A good soup can't be made in a hurry. You have to take your time. Do other things while the soup simmers and the time will pass quickly.

"The most important thing is to cook the soup long enough to have the vegetables just tender, not mushy and soft. You don't want to have a pot of mashed vegetables, right?"

For a meal, serve the soup accompanied by hot, buttered French bread or even plain crackers.

CORN OFF THE COB SOUP

MAKES ABOUT 2 GALLONS; SERVES ABOUT 16 (DEPENDING ON SERVING SIZE)

3 quarts water

3 pounds boneless beef sirloin roast, trimmed of fat and cut into 2-inch chunks

2 cups chopped yellow onions

1 cup chopped celery

One 8-ounce can tomato sauce

$3^{1}/_{2}$ cups cored and coarsely chopped white cabbage

$1^{1}/_{4}$ cups chopped carrots

1 cup chopped fresh tomatoes

3 cups peeled and cubed red potatoes (about 3 medium-size potatoes)

$^{1}/_{2}$ cup small, young, sweet peas

4 cups freshly cut corn kernels (from 6 to 8 ears of corn)

$^{1}/_{2}$ pound fresh green beans, ends trimmed and cut into 2-inch pieces

$^{1}/_{4}$ cup seeded and chopped red bell peppers

$^{1}/_{4}$ cup seeded and chopped green bell peppers

1 tablespoon salt

$^{1}/_{2}$ teaspoon freshly ground black pepper

$^{1}/_{2}$ teaspoon Tabasco brand pepper sauce

1. Combine the water and meat in a large, heavy pot or Dutch oven over medium heat. Bring to a boil, cover, reduce the heat to medium-low, and simmer for 45 minutes. Add the onions and celery and continue to simmer, covered, until the meat is tender, about 30 minutes.

2. Add the tomato sauce, cabbage, and carrots, cover, and continue to simmer for another 30 minutes.

3. Add the tomatoes, potatoes, peas, corn, beans, and red and green bell peppers, then stir in the salt, black pepper, and Tabasco. Cook, covered, stirring occasionally, until the meat and vegetables are tender, about 45 minutes. Serve hot, ladled into large soup bowls.

"It's time for a little history lesson. Listen well. Some say that the word jambalaya came from the French word *jambon* for ham, the African *ya* meaning rice, and the Acadian phrase *à la*. And you must understand that there are brown jambalayas, made by caramelizing and browning the onions and meats, and red ones, made by adding tomatoes. There are as many recipes for jambalaya as there are for gumbos in Louisiana. Personally, I like a bit of tomatoes in mine; I think it gives it a nice flavor. But, I'll let you taste, and then you can make up your own mind," Eula Mae says.

Jambalaya is also one of those popular Louisiana dishes that are very *apropos* for dining on the water. It's a one-pot meal, but you can serve it with a nice green salad and French bread.

When you're browning the chicken and ham, scrape the browned bits from the bottom of the pan. That gives the jambalaya a good flavor.

EULA MAE'S CHICKEN AND HAM JAMBALAYA

MAKES 6 TO 8 SERVINGS

1 fryer chicken (about 3 pounds), boned, skinned, and cut into 1-inch cubes, or $1^{1}/_{2}$ pounds skinless, boneless breasts and thighs, cut into 1-inch cubes

1 teaspoon salt

$^{1}/_{8}$ teaspoon freshly ground black pepper

$^{1}/_{8}$ teaspoon cayenne

2 tablespoons vegetable oil

$^{1}/_{2}$ pound cooked ham, cut into $^{1}/_{2}$-inch cubes

2 cups chopped yellow onions

1 cup seeded and chopped green bell peppers

1 cup chopped celery

4 garlic cloves, peeled

3 cups chicken broth

One 16-ounce can whole tomatoes, chopped, liquid reserved

$^{1}/_{2}$ cup chopped green onions (green part only)

2 tablespoons chopped fresh parsley leaves

2 pounds medium-size shrimp, peeled and deveined

1 teaspoon Tabasco brand pepper sauce

2 cups raw long-grain white rice, rinsed and drained

1. Sprinkle the chicken with the salt, black pepper, and cayenne. Heat the oil in a large, heavy pot or Dutch oven over medium heat. Add the chicken and cook, stirring, until browned on all sides, 8 to 10 minutes. Transfer the chicken to a large mixing bowl.

2. Add the ham to the pot and cook, stirring, until lightly browned, about 5 minutes. Add the ham to the chicken in the bowl.

3. Add the onions, bell peppers, celery, and garlic to the pot and cook, scraping the bottom of the pot to loosen any browned bits. Return the chicken and ham to the pot, reduce the heat to low, cover, and cook for 25 minutes, stirring occasionally.

4. Add the chicken broth and reserved tomato juice, cover, and simmer for 45 minutes.

5. Mash the cooked garlic against the side of the pot and blend into the mixture. Add the tomatoes, green onions, parsley, shrimp, and Tabasco and adjust the seasonings to taste. Add the rice, cover the pot, and bring to a boil. Reduce the heat to medium-low and simmer, covered, stirring occasionally, until the rice is tender and fluffy and the liquid is absorbed, about 25 minutes. Serve warm.

"**M**y husband and I used to dry shrimp and it was quite a process and a lot of work, but the dried shrimp could be used when we didn't have fresh shrimp to add to gumbos or stews. The dried shrimp have an intense flavor and can be cooked along with fresh shrimp to make this gumbo."

"To dry the shrimp, small or medium-size shrimp are first boiled in heavily salted water until the shell separates from the shrimp meat. The shrimp are then deheaded, then dried in screen boxes on the tin roof of a building in the sun. The boxes have legs so that the shrimp do not toughen on the hot tin. It usually is done when there's a dry north wind. The shrimp are raked and turned in the shallow boxes until the shells fly off. The shrimp must be turned often until they are perfectly dried. It was a lot of work and so hot, but when we wanted dried shrimp, we had to do it ourselves."

Indeed, the dried shrimp give this gumbo a very powerful taste. Dried shrimp and dried shrimp powder can be found in many Asian and Chinese markets. Of course, in south Louisiana, you'll find it in supermarkets, country grocery stores, seafood markets, and convenience stores.

The practice of poaching eggs in stews and gumbos has been around for a long, long time. Eggs were always plentiful because just about everyone had chickens. The eggs were often poached in meatless stews, like potato stew, to provide a heartier meal. Sometimes, hard-boiled eggs (peeled and finely chopped) are used to garnish shrimp stew, local Friday fare. The locals like to mash the eggs into the gravy to make it even thicker than it already is.

Eula Mae offers this tip about making gumbos: Be sure to add enough water when you begin cooking the gumbo. It's best not to add it during the cooking time.

DRIED SHRIMP AND EGG GUMBO

MAKES 8 SERVINGS

$^1/_2$ cup vegetable oil

$^2/_3$ cup all-purpose flour

1 cup chopped yellow onions

$^1/_4$ cup seeded and chopped green bell peppers

$^1/_4$ cup seeded and chopped red bell peppers

1 rib celery, chopped

2 garlic cloves, peeled

8 cups water

$\frac{1}{4}$ cup dried shrimp soaked in $\frac{1}{2}$ cup water for 1 hour

1 teaspoon salt

$\frac{1}{2}$ teaspoon freshly ground black pepper

$\frac{1}{2}$ teaspoon Accent seasoning

$\frac{1}{4}$ teaspoon Tabasco brand garlic pepper sauce

1 pound medium-size fresh shrimp, peeled and deveined

$\frac{1}{2}$ cup chopped green onions (green and white parts)

$\frac{1}{2}$ cup chopped fresh parsley leaves

8 large eggs

Hot cooked long-grain white rice (see page 171)

1. Heat the oil in a large, heavy pot over medium heat for 2 minutes. Add the flour and stir constantly to make a dark brown roux (see Eula Mae's advice on making a roux, page 94), the color of chocolate, 15 to 20 minutes. Add the onions and cook, stirring, for 1 minute. Add the bell peppers, celery, and garlic and cook, stirring, for 2 minutes. Add 2 cups of the water and stir to blend well. Add the remaining 6 cups water and stir again to blend. Drain the dried shrimp and add to the pot. Cover the pot, reduce the heat to medium-low, and simmer for 1½ hours.

2. Add the salt, black pepper, Accent, and Tabasco and skim off any oil that has risen to the surface. Drain off 4 cups of the gumbo liquid into a medium-size saucepan over medium heat. Return the gumbo pot with the remaining liquid and the vegetables to medium heat, add the fresh shrimp, green onions, and parsley, bring to a simmer, and let simmer, covered, for 10 to 15 minutes.

3. Meanwhile, put 1 egg in a cup and gently slide it into the saucepan containing just the gumbo liquid. Repeat with the remaining eggs, putting them in various places in the saucepan, not on top of each other. Poach until the whites are set and the yolks are just firm, about 5 minutes. Then, carefully, using a slotted spoon, lift them out and transfer them to the big pot of gumbo and let simmer, covered, for 10 to 15 minutes.

4. Serve in gumbo bowls or deep soup bowls with rice, each serving topped with one of the poached eggs.

Ti gâteau sec is French for little dry cakes. They are indeed nothing fancy since they are made with ingredients—flour, butter, sugar—that were available on the farms in the rural areas of Acadiana.

They were often made for young children when they came home from school. They can be accompanied with *café au lait* (coffee milk) made with equal parts strong, dark coffee and hot milk or cream. For a heartier snack or dessert, they were served with Creole cream cheese.

"Susan, my daughter, loved them. She and I would sit in the kitchen after school and, while she told me of her day, she'd eat them slowly and make them last longer!" says Eula Mae.

They are also ideal for packing in airtight containers to take along on a boat trip, or to a picnic or any outdoor meal. The dough can be made in advance and stored in an airtight container in the refrigerator for up to three days. This basic dough can be used for sweet tarts, sometimes referred to as turnovers, and can be filled with fig preserves, baked sliced apples, or blackberry jam.

TI GÂTEAU SEC

MAKES ABOUT 28 COOKIES

$1/2$ cup (1 stick) butter, at room temperature

$1/4$ teaspoon ground mace

$1/8$ teaspoon ground nutmeg

1 cup sugar

2 large eggs

1 teaspoon pure vanilla extract

$1/3$ cup evaporated milk

3 cups all-purpose flour

1 tablespoon baking powder

$1/8$ teaspoon salt

1. Cream together the butter, mace, nutmeg, and sugar in a large mixing bowl until soft and fluffy. Add the eggs and beat again until thick and smooth. Add the vanilla and beat again. Add the evaporated milk and blend.

2. In a medium-size mixing bowl, sift together the flour, baking powder, and salt. Add this to the butter mixture and stir in one direction with a wooden spoon until it is all incorporated. The dough will be thick and slightly sticky. Form it into a ball, wrap in plastic wrap, and chill for at least 1 hour.

3. Preheat the oven to 350°F. Line a baking sheet with parchment paper. Lightly dust a work surface with flour. Divide the dough into 2 equal portions. Gently pat one portion into a flattened ball and put it on the flour-dusted surface. With a lightly floured rolling pin, gently roll out the dough into a circle about 9 inches in diameter and ¼ inch thick. Cut the cookies with a 2-inch cookie cutter and place them on the prepared baking sheet about ½ inch apart. Gather up the scraps, roll them out, and cut more cookies. You should have about 14 cookies per portion of dough. Repeat with the remaining portion of dough.

4. Bake until lightly golden, about 15 minutes. Remove from the oven and let cool for about 5 minutes. Then, with a metal spatula, carefully lift the cookies off the pan and transfer them to a wire rack to cool completely.

> **VARIATION** To make tarts, simply roll out the dough into circles 6 to 8 inches in diameter and ¼ inch thick. Fill with about ¼ cup of the desired filling, fold the dough over, and seal. Press the edges together with the tines of a fork. Bake until lightly golden, 15 to 20 minutes.

Tart lemon pie is a favorite in south Louisiana.

Eula Mae told me one day, "You know, darling, lemons are available year-round, and I think a lemon pie is ideal to serve with seafood. The tartness of the citrus clears the taste buds, and it can be easily made ahead and carefully wrapped to take along anywhere."

During the winter, local citrus is available from the many groves southeast of New Orleans in the parishes of Plaquemines and St. Bernard in the fertile land near the mouth of the Mississippi River.

SOUTH LOUISIANA LEMON PIE

MAKES ONE 9-INCH PIE; SERVES 6

$^{1}/_{2}$ cup all-purpose flour

$^{1}/_{2}$ cup cornstarch

$2^{1}/_{4}$ cups plus 2 tablespoons sugar

2 cups water

4 large eggs, separated

1 cup fresh lemon juice

$^{1}/_{4}$ cup ($^{1}/_{2}$ stick) butter, cut into pieces

1 Basic Pie Crust (page 136), baked

$^{1}/_{4}$ teaspoon cream of tartar

$^{1}/_{2}$ teaspoon clear vanilla flavoring

1. Preheat the oven to 350°F.

2. Combine the flour, cornstarch, 2 cups of the sugar, and the water in a large, deep, heavy saucepan over medium heat. Beat the egg yolks together well, then whisk them into the flour mixture and continue to whisk until the mixture thickens. Add the lemon juice and butter and blend. Remove from the heat and let cool slightly. Pour into the prepared pie crust.

3. Using an electric mixer, beat the egg whites with the cream of tartar in a large mixing bowl until frothy. Gradually beat in the remaining $^{1}/_{4}$ cup plus 2 tablespoons sugar a little at a time and continue to beat until the whites are stiff and glossy. Beat in the vanilla. Spread

the meringue over the pie filling, being careful to spread to the edges of the crust, otherwise the filling will bubble up through the openings.

4. Bake until the meringue is delicately browned, 8 to 10 minutes. Remove from the oven and let cool completely before serving.

Creole Cream Cheese

Louisiana's Creole cream cheese is called Creole because the word means native and that is precisely what it is, native to New Orleans. Creole cream cheese is made from skim milk, buttermilk, and rennet (a product which causes the whey and curd to separate), resulting in a delicious and highly versatile custard-like cheese. In consistency and flavor, it's a bit like yogurt cheese, with a decided difference. Traditionally, this tart, single-curd cheese was made with clabbered milk, then hung in cheesecloth under the oak trees to drip whey. Literally every person carrying a few extra wrinkles remembers eating it as a kid. In turn, they remember their mother or grandmother making it. Most recall having Creole cream cheese for breakfast. Typically, the dish was served with fruit or topped with a small amount of cream and sprinkled with sugar. Some people also spoon Creole cream cheese on top of toast and sprinkle it with salt and pepper.

FALL

"After the summer garden peters out, usually by the middle of August, it's time to get ready to plant the fall garden. When I was young, Daddy always put in peanuts, carrots, mustard greens, and cabbage in our home garden. Of course, sweet potatoes and rice are large fall cash crops in south Louisiana, and we had plenty available to us. There is a large community garden on the Island,

and I often visit it to pick turnips and mustard greens in the fall. There is nothing better than vegetables straight from the soil."

Fall officially begins around September 22, but in south Louisiana it unofficially begins right after Labor Day. Children go back to school around the middle of August, and come September there's a hint of autumn air.

"I have a very sharp nose and I can sniff the changes, and know that the earth is preparing for shorter days and cooler weather," Eula Mae told me one cool afternoon in October.

You need only to study the landscape and notice the difference as the Island takes on a new appearance.

"*Chère*, just as people change the types of clothing as the seasons change, so does the scenery. See the delicate tiny leaves of the tall bald cypress trees. During spring and summer, they were bright green and now they are turning brown and drop gently in the wind. The willow trees begin shedding and soon the blue herons will move on to other nesting places."

Once again, we drive slowly along the narrow roads on the Island, taking note of the changes. Dusk is approaching as we creep along the banks of the Saline Woods.

"See the red eyes of a gator moving slowly in the middle of the water? Over there is a red-beaked marsh hen pecking for food. I hope the alligator doesn't see him! Oh, and look, *chère*, see the knobby cypress knees jutting out along the edge of the pond. If you look carefully, you can sometimes see shapes, like this one here. Doesn't it look like the profile of an old man with a beard? And here, this one looks like a very sad face. You can find so many things in nature if you look for them."

The light began to fade and darkness was setting in. A gray mist began to roll in from the marsh and the frogs and crickets began their evening concert—so loud, then ever so softly.

We turned our vehicle around and headed back to her house, nestled cozily under the moss-draped trees.

We inhaled deeply and got a strong whiff of the sugarcane burning in the fields. It is an odor we both know very well. This is sugarcane country, after all. During the harvest, called *la roulaison*, the cane is cut in the fields. The leaves on the stalks are removed by setting the cut cane on fire. The sweet-sour smell blankets the countryside. Once the cane is burned, it is loaded onto huge trucks that carry it to the sugar mills, where it is mashed, the sweet juice extracted, and boiled until it crystallizes. The raw sugar is then sent on to refineries. The sugar mills are large, sometimes three stories high, and are filled with cutting machines, huge vats, large tanks, and huge sugar warehouses. Think about that when you reach for the sugar for your morning coffee!

We passed the pepper fields, now vacant and quiet, where just weeks before, they had been alive and busy with pickers. The pepper harvest usually begins in late summer, as soon as the peppers ripen to the perfect shade of bright red, and can last until the weather turns cold.

"*Chère*, the peppers are picked by hand because machines wouldn't know the color of the peppers. You see, young peppers are green, turn yellow, then orange, and finally, bright red as they age. If the pickers are in doubt about the color, they have with them *le petit bâton rouge*, which is a small wooden dowel painted the preferred hue of the peppers. They can match the stick with the red peppers to see if the color is just right."

During pepper-picking season, the Island is busy. The same day the peppers are picked, they are mashed, mixed with a small amount of Avery Island salt, placed in white oak barrels, and allowed to ferment and then age for up to three years.

"The pungent aroma of the mashed peppers wafts on the breeze and it tickles my nose," says Eula Mae.

Until the late 1960s, all the peppers for the making of Tabasco brand pepper sauce were grown on the Island. But now more than 90 percent of the pepper crop is grown in Central and South America. The high quality of the next pepper crop on the Island is ensured by the McIlhennys, who personally select the best plants in the field during harvest. The pepper seeds from those select plants are treated and dried, and then stored for use the following year.

"Times have changed," remarks Eula Mae. "I can remember when all the bottles of Tabasco pepper sauce had to be hand capped, but now, there are machines that do that. But be assured, the sauce has never changed."

HALLOWEEN BONFIRE

Popcorn Balls

Halloween Hot Dogs with Chili and Homemade Bread

In 1953, MoNeg and Eula Mae began a tradition that continues today.

"We always loved to have children around us. Near our house was an area that was used by the Boy Scouts for a campground. One Halloween, MoNeg suggested that we have a bonfire there. He was always thinking of something fun to do."

It began with only about fifteen people—parents with their children—but now over two hundred attend. A few years ago, so many people arrived at the gate, some had to be turned away. The bill of fare has always been hot dogs, corn chips, roasted marshmallows, soft drinks, and, of course, candy.

"I always get up early and put the chili cooking, then let it simmer for the better part of the day. The wieners are put at the end of bamboo sticks, since we have lots of bamboo on the Island, and are roasted on an open pit of burning charcoal and wood. The wieners are then plopped on a warm bun with a scoop of the chili. Then, sometimes we have small bags of Fritos. We open them and put a scoop of chili in the bag! What a treat! Sometimes we all go trick-or-treating on the Island, winding our way through the dense wooded areas, watching the moon rise, and enjoying time with the families. I wouldn't miss it for the world!" she exclaims.

"Sometimes we all go trick-or-treating on the Island,

winding our way through the dense wooded areas, watching

the moon rise, and enjoying time with the families."

"**P**opping popcorn brings back many memories. Years ago, before television, some of our friends would join my husband and me and, with our children, sit at the kitchen table and munch on freshly popped popcorn. We would talk, exchange gossip, and play with the kids. Now that is what I believe is quality time!"

Eula Mae has made thousands and thousands of popcorn balls for just about all occasions, but especially for the Halloween party. They can be wrapped in waxed paper and put on a tray, and guests can pick them up whenever they want.

When the weather is cold and a north wind is blowing, the popcorn sticks together better. You'll notice these are made with syrup made from sugarcane! Having a candy thermometer will make this a piece of cake.

POPCORN BALLS

MAKES 12 TO 14 BALLS

1 tablespoon peanut oil
$1/4$ cup popping corn kernels
$1^1/2$ cups cane syrup
$1/2$ cup firmly packed dark brown sugar

1. Heat the oil in a heavy, medium-size saucepan over medium heat. Add the corn kernels and swirl to make sure the kernels are evenly coated with the oil and are in a single layer. Cover the pot and gently shake until the popping stops. Carefully remove the lid and transfer the popcorn to a large bowl.

2. Combine the syrup and brown sugar in a heavy, medium-size saucepan. Heat the mixture over medium-low heat and stir to dissolve the sugar. Stir constantly while cooking. Do not leave it alone; cook until it reaches the thread stage (see page 15), when the temperature is 270° to 290°F. It will be the color of taffy and thick.

3. Carefully pour the syrup over the popped corn. Stir with a long-handled spoon to coat evenly. Once it's coated evenly and cooled a bit, break off the popcorn and form into balls about the size of a baseball, or as big or little as you want. Place on a layer of waxed paper to cool. When cooled completely, wrap in waxed paper.

When Eula Mae offered to make this chili one day in the test kitchen, she explained that she had never given out her recipe.

She whispered, "You will be the first person to see what I do to make this chili so good. I have never revealed this recipe to anyone, except my daughter, in fifty years. Adding the chili powder mixed with some flour is the secret to making the chili just right. You'll see what I mean when you try it."

First of all, the chili must simmer for several hours. It can't be rushed. Put it on early in the morning and let it cook long and slow. Eula Mae usually has to use about forty pounds of ground beef for the crowds that now number over two hundred, so the process takes her all day.

CHILI FOR HALLOWEEN HOT DOGS

MAKES ABOUT 1¹/₂ QUARTS CHILI

1 tablespoon vegetable oil

2 pounds ground beef

1 teaspoon salt

1 teaspoon freshly ground black pepper

¹/₄ teaspoon Tabasco brand pepper sauce

¹/₂ teaspoon Accent seasoning

3 cups chopped yellow onions

2 cups chopped celery

1 cup seeded and chopped green bell peppers

4 garlic cloves, peeled

One 6-ounce can tomato paste

2 tablespoons chili powder

¹/₄ cup all-purpose flour

1 cup water

1. Heat the oil in a large, heavy pot over medium heat. Add the beef, salt, pepper, Tabasco, and Accent and cook, stirring, until all the pink disappears. Add the onions, celery, bell peppers, and garlic and cook, stirring, until the onions are soft and lightly golden, about 10 minutes. Add the tomato paste and 1 tablespoon of the chili powder and mix well. Cook, covered, stirring occasionally, over very low heat for at least 2 hours and as long as 3 hours.

2. Combine the remaining 1 tablespoon chili powder with the flour in a small bowl and blend well, then add the water and stir to mix. Add to the pot of chili and cook, stirring, for about 1 minute.

3. Turn off the heat and let sit for about 15 minutes, stirring occasionally, before serving.

"I can't make buns for a large crowd, but hot dog buns made from my home-made bread would be *très bon* if you have only a few people," explains Eula Mae. "You can also make 'pull-apart' bread with this recipe, which children, and even a lot of adults, adore. You put little balls of dough close together on a baking sheet so that they can rise and bake close together. Then you simply pull the little balls apart and munch on them. And you must have butter, real butter, to spread on the bread."

HOMEMADE BREAD

MAKES 2 BIG LOAVES, ABOUT 30 SMALL PULL-APARTS,
OR 12 SMALL BAGUETTES ABOUT 4 INCHES LONG AND
1 TO 2 INCHES IN DIAMETER

2 cups warm water (about 110°F)
One $\frac{1}{4}$-ounce envelope active dry yeast
1 tablespoon sugar
2 tablespoons vegetable oil
1 teaspoon salt
5 cups plus 1 tablespoon all-purpose flour
1 tablespoon cornmeal
$\frac{1}{4}$ cup ($\frac{1}{2}$ stick) butter, melted

1. Put 1 cup of the warm water in a large mixing bowl, then sprinkle the yeast over it. Stir to dissolve the yeast, then add the remaining 1 cup water. Add the sugar and oil and blend. Add the salt and 4 cups of the flour and mix well. Cover with a damp towel and set aside in a warm, draft-free place until the dough doubles in size, about 1 hour.

2. Sprinkle 1 cup of the remaining flour over the risen dough, then invert it onto a lightly floured surface. Knead it until soft and elastic. Return it to the bowl, cover with a damp cloth, and let it rise until it doubles in size again and puffs over the sides of the bowl, about 1 hour.

3. Sprinkle a work surface with the remaining 1 tablespoon flour and the cornmeal. Turn the dough out onto the prepared surface.

At this point, you can divide the dough into 2 equal portions to make 2 long loaves. Or catch up enough dough, about the size of a large egg, roll it a bit in your hands, and pat it into the shape of a small French bread, 3 to 4 inches long, which will make an ideal hot dog bun. Or shape egg-size pieces of dough into 2-inch balls.

For the large loaves, roll each portion of the dough into the shape of a baguette, about 12 inches long and 2 to 3 inches in diameter. Place them on a nonstick or lightly oiled baking sheet. Cover with plastic wrap and put in a warm, draft-free place to let rise for 30 minutes. Or cover with plastic wrap and refrigerate for as long as several hours.

Follow the same procedure to make smaller loaves.

For the "pull-apart" bread, after patting the dough into small rounds, place them crowded together on the pan before covering to let rise or to refrigerate.

4. Preheat the oven 400°F.

5. Bake until lightly golden, about 20 minutes. Remove from the oven and brush the tops lightly with the melted butter before serving.

FALL HARVEST

Shrimp Potato Patties

Mini Oyster Tarts

Eula Mae's Shrimp Creole

Homemade Gingersnap "Cakes"

Les Oreilles de Cochon

Sweet Potato Pie

Eula Mae's Pecan Pie

Besides being the time of the sugarcane harvest, fall is the season for festivals and celebrations honoring crops, food, and music. The town of Rayne honors *Monsieur Grenouille* (Mr. Frog). Local legend tells us that a chef named Donat Pucheu started selling juicy, delectable bullfrogs from the Rayne area to New Orleans restaurants and word spread like wildfire. Rayne, located in what is known as Louisiana's Cajun prairie in the southwestern area of the state, was named the Frog Capital of the World when, in the 1940s, the townspeople held a Frog Derby. The prettiest ladies in town dressed frogs in jockey uniforms and raced them. The event continues to this day. Although Rayne no longer exports frogs, the town continues to honor Mr. Frog with large murals as well as paintings of frogs on trees, walls, and fences.

In Plaisance, the Southwest Louisiana Zydeco Music Festival offers many bands playing from morning until night. Shrimp and oil are celebrated in Morgan City at the Louisiana Shrimp & Petroleum Festival. There are also festivals to pay tribute to rice and yams. *Festivals Acadiens* is actually three festivals in one—Louisiana Native & Contemporary Crafts Festival, the Bayou Food Festival, and the *Festival de Musique Acadienne*.

And if that's not enough to keep everyone occupied, the men of south Louisiana are preparing for the hunting season. There are always many guests who come to the Island to participate in the hunts.

"Let's see, around Labor Day, they go after alligators, then they will be going to their duck and deer hunting camps. Oh, my, those men get so excited. And I do too! There is nothing better than roasted ducks, or duck gumbo, or even wild game jambalaya! Oh, and then there will be fishing trips to nearby Vermilion Bay and even the Gulf of Mexico. Ah, I can almost taste fresh catfish and garfish, or perhaps even speckled trout! Of course, the shrimp and crab season will be getting into full swing! My, aren't we fortunate to have such good things right at our door?"

"There is nothing better

than roasted ducks, or

duck gumbo, or even wild

game jambalaya!"

Did you know that the Acadians came to Louisiana in the late eighteenth century from Nova Scotia, which was then called Acadie? Thus the evolution of the term Acadian, *'cadien*, Cajun. Hunters, trappers, and farmers in the mid- to late eighteenth century, when the British assumed control of the French territory, refused to change their allegiance and were expelled from their beloved land. Some went to France, while others found their way to south Louisiana, where they hoped to find a new home among fellow Frenchmen who had settled there.

"Can you imagine, *chère*, how sad it must have been to leave their homes? But they had great faith and a *joie de vivre*, a joy of living that shows in their style of cooking. Take, for example, these simple shrimp patties. The ingredients are nothing more than potatoes, fresh shrimp, flour, onions, bell peppers, all of which were at hand. But they are so tasty and fun. Every time I serve them, I get rave reviews. They are wonderful to serve at luncheons as a main course, or as a side dish to just about anything. You can substitute crabmeat or crawfish for the shrimp."

SHRIMP POTATO PATTIES

MAKES ABOUT 2 DOZEN (DEPENDING ON THE SIZE)

6 medium-size red potatoes, peeled and quartered

$^1/_2$ cup (1 stick) butter

1 cup finely chopped yellow onions

$^1/_4$ cup chopped celery

$^1/_2$ cup seeded and chopped red bell peppers

$^1/_2$ cup seeded and chopped green bell peppers

$^1/_2$ cup seeded and chopped yellow bell peppers

$^3/_4$ teaspoon salt

$^1/_4$ teaspoon cayenne

$^1/_4$ teaspoon freshly ground black pepper

$^1/_4$ teaspoon Tabasco brand pepper sauce

2 pounds medium-size shrimp, peeled, deveined, and coarsely ground in a food processor

2 large eggs, well beaten

$^1/_4$ cup chopped fresh parsley leaves

$^1/_2$ cup peanut oil

$^1/_2$ cup all-purpose flour

1. In a large saucepan, boil the potatoes in lightly salted water to cover until fork tender. Remove from the heat and drain. Transfer them to a large mixing bowl and mash with a fork. Let cool.

2. Melt the butter over medium heat in a medium-size skillet. Add the onions, celery, bell peppers, salt, cayenne, black pepper, and Tabasco and cook, stirring, until soft, about 5 minutes. Add the shrimp and cook, stirring, until they turn pink, about 3 minutes. Remove from the heat and let cool for about 5 minutes.

3. Combine the shrimp mixture with the potato mixture. Add the eggs and parsley and mix well. Let cool for 10 minutes.

4. Heat the oil in a large skillet over medium heat.

5. Form the shrimp mixture into patties, using $\frac{1}{4}$ to $\frac{1}{2}$ cup of the mixture, depending on what size you desire, and pat lightly with the flour. Cook two to three at a time in the hot oil until golden brown, about 3 minutes on each side. Drain on paper towels. Serve hot.

During the fall and winter, when the waters in the bays along the Gulf of Mexico are cold, oyster luggers are busy at work. The oyster fishermen work year-round. The oyster beds along the coastline must be seeded and reseeded year after year with oyster shells. When the oysters have grown and matured, they are harvested. This is backbreaking work. The men on the luggers haul up heavy nets and baskets filled with the oysters in their shells. Then the oysters are sorted, iced down, and quickly sent to market.

History tells us that Aristotle and Lucullus were fond of the mollusk and that fishermen at Rhodes were wont to throw potsherds into the bays to provide housing for oyster "spat." Spat are young, floating oysters, which attach themselves to oysters shells and artificial beds. Oysters are so productive (thus the aphrodisiac reputation) that a single female may lay some five million eggs at a time, but in the wild only ten to fifteen single eggs are likely to survive.

It is then not surprising that Louisiana colonists, those brave souls, were thrilled to find an abundance of oysters in the bays and estuaries along the coast of the Gulf of Mexico.

"When they are in season, I use them as often as I can. These tarts are very popular at just about any function we have on the Island, especially at cocktail parties at this time of the year."

You can find small prepared patty shells, about three inches in diameter, in the frozen food section at most supermarkets. Smaller bite-size shells are often available at bakery shops.

Before seasoning the mixture, taste the oysters. They are often quite salty and you don't want to overseason.

MINI OYSTER TARTS

MAKES 1 DOZEN 3-INCH PATTIES OR 3 DOZEN SMALL PATTIES

$^1/_2$ cup vegetable oil

$^3/_4$ cup all-purpose flour

$2^1/_2$ cups chopped yellow onions

$^1/_2$ cup seeded and chopped green bell peppers

$^1/_2$ cup seeded and chopped red bell peppers

2 garlic cloves, pressed

$^1/_2$ cup sliced white button mushrooms

$^1/_2$ cup (1 stick) butter

1 quart oysters, well drained and liquor reserved

Salt, white pepper, and freshly ground black pepper to taste

$^1/_8$ teaspoon Tabasco brand pepper sauce

3 tablespoons finely chopped fresh parsley leaves

2 tablespoons finely chopped green onions (green part only)

1 dozen 3-inch patty shells or 36 bite-size patty shells

1. Heat the oil for 2 minutes in a large, heavy saucepan over medium heat. Add the flour, blend, and cook, stirring constantly and slowly, to make a roux the color of peanut butter (see Eula Mae's advice on making a roux, page 94). Add the onions and cook, stirring, until very soft, about 15 minutes. Add the bell peppers, garlic, mushrooms, and butter and cook, stirring, for 5 minutes. Add the reserved oyster liquor and reduce the heat to medium-low. Simmer, stirring often, until the mixture thickens. Add the oysters, season with salt, white pepper, black pepper, and Tabasco, and cook until the edges of the oysters just begin to curl. Remove from the heat. Stir in the parsley and green onions. Let cool to room temperature.

2. Preheat the oven to 350°F.

3. Fill the patty shells about three quarters full with the filling. Put them on an ungreased baking sheet and bake until golden, 20 to 25 minutes. Serve immediately.

ecause shrimp are plentiful during late summer and early fall, they are prepared in many different ways. When Eula Mae told me she wanted me to taste her shrimp Creole, I grimaced. I have had some bad, really bad shrimp Creoles in the past and I was a little hesitant. But I should have known better.

"You are going to like mine," she said with a laugh. "Some versions have too many tomatoes and they're not cooked properly. Be careful when cooking with any kind of tomatoes. You don't want to scorch them and cause the dish to have a burnt taste. It's my opinion that this dish has to cook slowly in the beginning so that the roux and the vegetables can cook together. Here is one of those times when I put the garlic cloves in the pot whole and, when they get soft—I call it melting—you know the mixture in the pot has cooked long enough! When the garlic is very soft, it really does just about melt. Well, sometimes I give it a little nudge and press it against the side of the pot with a spoon."

EULA MAE'S SHRIMP CREOLE

MAKES 6 SERVINGS

$1/4$ cup vegetable oil

$1/4$ cup all-purpose flour

$1^1/2$ cups chopped yellow onions

2 large garlic cloves, peeled

$1/3$ cup chopped celery

$1/3$ cup seeded and chopped green bell peppers

$1/3$ cup seeded and chopped red bell peppers

One 16-ounce can tomato sauce

$1/3$ cup chopped fresh parsley leaves

$1/4$ cup chopped green onions (green and white parts)

1 teaspoon salt

$1/2$ teaspoon freshly ground black pepper

1 teaspoon Tabasco brand pepper sauce

3 pounds medium-size shrimp, peeled and deveined

$1/2$ cup water

6 cups hot cooked long-grain white rice (see page 171)

1. Heat the oil for 2 minutes in a large, heavy pot over medium heat. Add the flour, blend, and cook, stirring slowly and constantly, to make a roux the color of peanut butter, 5 to 6 minutes (see Eula Mae's advice on making a roux, page 94). Add the onions and cook, stirring often, until they are just soft, about 5 minutes. Add the garlic and cook for 2 minutes, stirring. Add the celery and bell peppers and cook, stirring, for 3 to 4 minutes. Add the tomato sauce and stir to mix. Cover, reduce the heat to medium-low, and simmer, stirring occasionally, until the garlic melts, the vegetables are very soft, and the mixture is very thick, about 45 minutes.

2. Add the parsley and green onions and stir to mix well, scraping the side and bottom of the pan. Add the salt, black pepper, and Tabasco and stir to mix. Add the shrimp and water and stir to mix. Cover and simmer, stirring occasionally, until the mixture is thick and smooth, 20 to 25 minutes. Serve hot over steamed rice.

"During the sugarcane season, Daddy often bartered with his farmer friends for raw sugar, cane syrup, or the dark, thick molasses from the sugar mills. We often made these little cakes. And later, when my daughter, Susan, was little, we made these for after-school treats. They are simple, but the molasses gives these a special taste that brings many good memories of when I was growing up."

A gingerbread man cookie cutter can be used, but Eula Mae says that when she was a little girl they didn't have cookie cutters.

"We cut them out by hand. We used raisins for their eyes, but when my daughter was young, we sometimes used red hot candy or colored sugar to decorate the gingerbread men. Sometimes we made a half-moon or a star, whatever we could create. Of course, you can cut out regular cookies by using a cookie cutter or a glass or cup. And remember, in the old days, we baked in a wood stove, so we had no idea at what temperature they were to be baked!"

HOMEMADE GINGERSNAP "CAKES"

MAKES ABOUT 1 DOZEN (DEPENDING ON SIZE OF COOKIES)

$1/4$ cup pure, natural, dark molasses (unsulfured)

$1/4$ cup firmly packed dark brown sugar

1 tablespoon butter, at room temperature

$1^1/2$ tablespoons very cold water

$1^1/2$ cups all-purpose flour

$1/4$ teaspoon baking soda

$1/8$ teaspoon salt

$1/4$ teaspoon ground ginger

$1/8$ teaspoon ground allspice

$1/8$ teaspoon ground cloves

$1/8$ teaspoon ground cinnamon

1. Preheat the oven to 350°F.

2. Combine the molasses, brown sugar, butter, and water in a large mixing bowl. Stir to blend with a spoon; don't use an electric mixer. In a medium-size mixing bowl, combine the flour, baking soda, salt, and spices. Add the dry mixture to the wet and stir together well. It will make a very dry, stiff dough.

3. On a very lightly floured work surface, roll the dough out to about ¼-inch thickness and cut out figures or cookies with a cookie cutter. Place them about 1 inch apart on an ungreased baking sheet.

4. Bake until the cookies are just firm to the touch and begin to color around the edges, 8 to 10 minutes. Do not overbake.

These little pastries are south Louisiana favorites. They were often prepared as after-school treats for children, especially during the fall when the weather is cold. The name translates literally as "pig's ears" because that's what they look like after they are fried. The cane syrup is what makes them so yummy!

This recipe is for a small amount, but you can double or triple it.

LES OREILLES DE COCHON

MAKES ABOUT 1 DOZEN

2 cups all-purpose flour

2 teaspoons baking powder

$1/8$ teaspoon baking soda

1 teaspoon salt

1 tablespoon sugar

$1/2$ cup milk

3 cups vegetable oil

1 cup Steen's 100% Pure Cane Syrup

1. Combine the flour, baking powder, baking soda, salt, and sugar in a medium-size mixing bowl and blend. Make a well in the center of the dry ingredients and add the milk. Stir in one direction with a wooden spoon until all the dry ingredients are incorporated and the dough comes together into a ball.

2. Transfer the dough to a lightly floured work surface. Lightly flour your hands, pick up the dough, and pat it into a flattened ball. Divide the dough into equal portions and form into balls about the size of Ping-Pong balls. With your fingers, flatten the balls out into circles about 3 inches in diameter and $1/4$ inch thick. (Alternately, you can roll them out with a rolling pin.)

3. Heat the oil in a large, deep pot or an electric fryer to 360°F.

4. Add one of the pastry pieces to the hot oil and, using the tines of a long-handled fork, fold the dough over as it fries to resemble a pig's ear. Hold the fork in the dough until the form takes hold. Fry until lightly golden, then drain on paper towels. Repeat the process with the remaining pastry. Once they're all fried, transfer the ears to a baking sheet or tray lined with parchment or waxed paper.

5. In a heavy, medium-size saucepan, cook the cane syrup over medium-low heat, stirring, until it reaches the soft-ball stage, 234° to 240°F on a candy thermometer (see page 15). Drizzle the syrup over the ears. Serve warm or at room temperature.

You might have heard sweet potatoes called yams. Let's see if we can explain. The sweet potato and the yam belong to different botanical families, but are often confused as they are similar in appearance and texture and are frequently cooked in similar ways. In the 1800s, sweet potatoes were called *nyam* in the United States, after an African tuber akin to the sweet potato. In the 1930s, as a marketing strategy, Louisiana dubbed its orange sweet potatoes "yams" to differentiate them from a paler sweet potato grown in the Northeast.

"Well, whatever," said Eula Mae when we discussed them. "The sweet potatoes grown in south Louisiana are delicious, and that's all I need to know. I love to see the syrup ooze from the sweet potatoes as they bake in the oven. And the aroma of them baking is wonderful."

Sweet potatoes can be cooked in any number of ways—in casseroles, fried, in puddings and cakes. But Eula Mae likes this sweet potato pie. Mr. Paul says this is one of his favorites too. If you can't find fresh sweet potatoes, use canned, but be sure to drain them well before using.

SWEET POTATO PIE

MAKES ONE 9-INCH PIE; SERVES 6

3 large sweet potatoes, peeled and cut into 2-inch cubes

$1/4$ cup ($1/2$ stick) butter, cut into chips

3 large eggs, well beaten

$1/2$ cup pure, natural, dark molasses (unsulfured)

$1/4$ cup honey

$1/2$ cup sugar

$1/4$ teaspoon salt

$1/4$ teaspoon ground cinnamon

$1/4$ teaspoon ground allspice

$1/8$ teaspoon ground nutmeg

$1/8$ teaspoon ground mace

1 teaspoon grated orange zest

$1/2$ cup half-and-half

1 recipe Basic Pie Crust (page 136)

$3/4$ cup pecan halves

1. Preheat the oven to 425°F.

2. Put the sweet potatoes in a large, heavy pot and add enough water to cover. Bring to a boil, then let boil until tender and drain. Transfer the potatoes to a large mixing bowl and mash well with a fork while they are still hot. (You should have about 2 cups.) Add the butter chips and stir until all are melted. Add the eggs, molasses, honey, sugar, salt, spices, orange zest, and half-and-half and mix together well. Pour into the prepared pie crust and smooth the top with a rubber spatula. Arrange the pecan halves evenly over the top of the pie.

3. Bake for 15 minutes. Reduce the oven temperature to 350°F and bake until the pie is set and the pecans are toasted, 35 to 40 minutes. Remove from the oven and let cool at least 10 minutes. Serve warm or at room temperature.

❝I always find that it's best to chill the flour and the vegetable shortening before I make my pie crust. It is so warm and damp in south Louisiana that cool ingredients help to make the pie crust flakier and not tough. And you must never, never overwork the pastry. Be gentle and you will have a flaky, tender crust," advises Eula Mae.

Basic Pie Crust
MAKES ONE 9-INCH PIE CRUST

1¹/₂ cups all-purpose flour

1 teaspoon salt

1 tablespoon sugar

³/₄ cup vegetable shortening

1 large egg, well beaten

3 tablespoons ice cold water, or more as needed

1. Sift the flour, salt, and sugar into a medium-size mixing bowl. Add the shortening and work it in with your fingertips until the mixture resembles coarse crumbs. Combine the egg with the cold water and add to the dough mixture. Work the dough with your hands until it forms a smooth ball. (You may have to add another tablespoon of cold water.) Wrap the dough with plastic wrap and chill for 1 hour.

2. Remove the dough from the refrigerator and place it on a lightly floured work surface. With a lightly floured rolling pin, roll it out to about 12 inches in diameter and ¹/₄ inch thick. Carefully transfer it to a 9-inch pie pan. Flute the edges.

In the north central part of Louisiana, there are many pecan orchards where tons of nuts are harvested during the fall and winter. But pecan trees grow wild practically all over the state and, of course, on the Island. When the first cold front moves in, the leaves on the pecan trees turn brown and dry, then the nuts fall to the ground. In yards and along country roads, people can be seen on all fours, gathering the prized nuts. Some are sold; most are kept for home use.

"During the fall, we pick pecans and always shell them to store in the freezer to use in pies and other desserts. Most people make pecan pies with pecan halves. But I've been making this one, with ground pecans, for years and it's become my signature pie! I think you'll like the difference in the texture."

Ground pecans are available at some stores in Louisiana, but you can grind them up yourself in a food processor. They should be as fine as bread crumbs.

EULA MAE'S PECAN PIE

MAKES ONE 9-INCH PIE; SERVES 6

2 tablespoons butter, softened

¾ cup sugar

3 large eggs

¾ cup light corn syrup

2 cups ground pecans

1 tablespoon clear vanilla flavoring

1 recipe Basic Pie Crust (opposite page)

1. Preheat the oven to 350°F.

2. Cream the butter and sugar together in a large mixing bowl. Add the eggs and whisk to blend well. Add the corn syrup, pecans, and vanilla and mix well. Pour into the prepared pie crust. Bake until the pie puffs and is golden, about 45 minutes.

3. Remove from the oven and let cool. The pie will deflate a bit as it cools.

A FAMILY THANKSGIVING FEAST

Spinach Salad with Zesty Orange Dressing

Roasted Chicken

Cornbread Dressing

Sweet Potatoes Rolled in Raw Sugar

Minted Carrots with Cream

Chocolate Bread Pudding

Old-Fashioned Nut Cake

"Although we celebrated Thanksgiving when I was a young girl, it wasn't nearly the big affair that it is these days. Some of our relatives who lived nearby would sometimes join us. They might bring a side dish to go along with whatever our family had, which was usually roasted chicken or a pork roast. Since we didn't raise turkeys, they weren't on our menu. Everything, and I mean everything, came from the farm. We had canned vegetables in our pantry. Milk, butter, and cream came from the cows, and we, of course, had chickens, ducks, geese, and pigs. We rarely bought anything at the grocery store."

Later, when Eula Mae and MoNeg lived on the Island, they usually had a fairly quiet Thanksgiving Day.

"I only have two brothers—my sister died some time ago—and MoNeg had only one sister, but we all got together when we could. When we were still young, there weren't many children. Again, the meal was good, but nothing fancy. I suppose because we eat well all during the year, we just do the same thing on the holidays!"

The week before Thanksgiving is always hectic for everyone, but Eula Mae generously put aside a day for me in her busy schedule. We once again went for a walk along the narrow roads on the Island.

"Every day I thank God for all that He has given me, but at Thanksgiving, I'm especially grateful. You see, living on Avery Island is like enjoying a bit of Paradise. Although most of the grounds are carefully tended, there's a great deal that's left in the wild. Walking, or driving, around the Island, you'll see deer that will not be spooked; in fact, some will actually let you come right up to them. There are rabbits, and waterfowl, like mallards, teals, wild geese, as well as egrets, herons, ibis, and roseate spoonbills that consider this tranquil area their home. Every once in a while, we see small black bears, native to this area, in the wooded areas. It always amazes me that with all the activity on the Island, the animals come and go as they please, without disrupting anyone.

"But I am always appreciative of the food we have for our table, especially on Thanksgiving when all the families gather for a feast. The food may be simple, but it's always delicious!"

"Every day I thank God for all that He has given me, but at Thanksgiving, I'm especially grateful."

Eula Mae, used to canned or frozen spinach, discovered fresh spinach in the supermarket a few years ago and, always open to new ingredients, tried it in salads. There is spinach salad and then there is Eula Mae's spinach salad.

"I think just about everyone likes spinach salad. I watched other cooks do theirs, then I tried a lot of different combinations to make mine a little more interesting. The cubed ham, grapes, and cantaloupe make it quite hearty and very attractive."

SPINACH SALAD WITH ZESTY ORANGE DRESSING

MAKES 6 TO 8 SERVINGS

8 cups fresh spinach leaves, washed, stems trimmed, and patted dry

2 cups cubed boiled ham

1 small red onion, finely chopped

1 cup each green and red grapes, rinsed in cool water and patted dry

1 cup seeded cantaloupe cut into small dice

1 recipe Zesty Orange Dressing (recipe follows)

1 cup coarsely chopped pecans, lightly toasted (see Note)

1. Combine the spinach, ham, onion, grapes, and cantaloupe in a large salad bowl. Cover and refrigerate for about 30 minutes.

2. When ready to serve, pour the salad dressing over the mixture, then sprinkle with the pecans. Do not toss or else the spinach will wilt. Serve immediately.

NOTE To toast pecans, preheat the oven to 250°F, place the pecans in a shallow baking pan or rimmed baking sheet and bake until fragrant, about 15 minutes.

Zesty Orange Dressing

MAKES ABOUT $^3/_4$ CUP

1 tablespoon distilled white vinegar

$^1/_2$ cup extra virgin olive oil

1 tablespoon fresh orange juice

1 teaspoon grated orange zest

1 teaspoon salt

1 teaspoon white pepper

1 garlic clove, pressed

1. Combine all the ingredients together in a jar fitted with a lid and shake to mix well.

2. Chill until ready to serve. The dressing will keep in an airtight container for 3 days in the refrigerator.

If the men have a good hunt, roasted wild ducks or geese may appear on the celebration table, but Thanksgiving dinner in south Louisiana usually centers around roasted chicken or turkey. Simple? Yes! Good? You bet!

"I can't tell you how many people ask me how to roast a chicken. It's so simple, really. Cooking a chicken, small or large, or a turkey, like this will always give you a moist bird. I like to put one or two bay leaves or sprigs of parsley underneath the breast skin; not only does it give some flavor, but it makes it pretty if the bird is brought to the table to carve. It takes just a little tender loving care to show your family and guests you've taken the time to make the bird a little nicer.

"If you wish to cook a turkey, simply double the ingredients. I give the ingredients for a six-pound roasting chicken and I don't like to cook too large a turkey. One weighing about ten pounds is what I usually prepare."

You will have to adjust the cooking time for a larger bird.

ROASTED CHICKEN

MAKES ABOUT 8 SERVINGS

1 roasting chicken (about 6 pounds)

2 teaspoons salt

$1/4$ teaspoon cayenne

$1/4$ teaspoon white pepper

$1/4$ teaspoon freshly ground black pepper

$1/4$ teaspoon Accent seasoning

2 tablespoons butter

1 tablespoon Kitchen Bouquet seasoning

$1/2$ cup water

1 teaspoon all-purpose flour, or more as needed

1. Preheat the oven to 350°F.

2. Clean the bird well inside and out under cool running water. Pat dry with paper towels. Combine the salt, cayenne, white and black pepper, and Accent in a small bowl and blend. (The seasoning mixture can be doubled for a turkey or other larger bird.) Season the entire bird with the mixture, putting some between the skin and breast meat, and in the cavity, and rubbing it onto the skin.

3. Combine the butter and Kitchen Bouquet in a small saucepan and heat for 30 seconds. Rub (or brush) the outside of the chicken as well as the cavity with the mixture.

4. Put the chicken, breast side down, in a roasting pan, cover, and bake for 1 hour. Remove the pan from the oven, turn the chicken breast side up, and return to the oven. Cover and bake until the juices run clear and the drumsticks pull easily away from the body, 45 minutes to 1 hour.

5. Transfer the chicken to a platter and drain off any excess fat. Add the water to the pan and deglaze, stirring to remove any browned bits. (Eula Mae calls these browned bits *les grimilles*.) Add the flour to the pan juices and whisk to blend. Allow the chicken to rest for about 10 minutes before carving.

6. While carving, return the pan with the pan juices to cook about 5 minutes longer in the oven. Use the pan drippings to pour over the carved chicken.

In south Louisiana, dressings sometimes called stuffings are made with cornbread. The dressings, or stuffings, can be made with chicken, oysters, shrimp, ground beef, or sausage. The dressings can be used to stuff turkey or chicken, but most often they are served as a side dish.

"There are some people who just can't seem to make a good cornbread dressing, but I think you'll find it so easy. I don't like cornbread dressing that's too moist, but if you prefer it softer, add a little more broth to the mixture."

CORNBREAD DRESSING

MAKES 8 TO 10 SERVINGS

1 fryer (about 3^1/$_2$ pounds), with the giblets and neck, rinsed in cool water

3 tablespoons vegetable oil

1 cup finely chopped yellow onions

1 cup seeded and finely chopped green bell peppers

1 cup finely chopped celery

4 cups crumbled Country Cornbread (page 146)

^{1}/$_2$ cup chopped fresh parsley leaves

1 large egg, lightly beaten

1 large hard-boiled egg, peeled and finely chopped

1 teaspoon baking powder

^{1}/$_2$ teaspoon salt

^{1}/$_4$ teaspoon freshly ground black pepper

^{1}/$_4$ cup (^{1}/$_2$ stick) butter (optional), melted

1. Cut the fryer into serving pieces and coarsely chop the giblets. Place in a large, heavy stockpot or Dutch oven and add enough water to cover the chicken. Bring to a boil over high heat, then reduce the heat to medium-low and cover. Simmer until the chicken is falling off the bones, about 1 hour. Remove from the heat. Strain in a colander, reserving the chicken broth. Set the chicken and broth aside to cool.

2. When the chicken is cool enough to handle, pick the meat off the bones and discard the skin. Finely chop the chicken pieces, giblets, and liver. Pick the meat off the neck. Combine in a large mixing bowl.

3. Heat the oil in a large saucepan over medium heat. Add the onions, bell peppers, and celery and cook, stirring, until tender and golden, 6 to 8 minutes. Add the cornbread, parsley, and about ¾ cup of the chicken broth.

4. In a small mixing bowl, combine the beaten egg, hard-boiled egg, and baking powder. Mix well, then add to the cornbread mixture. Add the chicken pieces and salt and pepper. Mix gently. Add more broth if you want it to be moister. The mixture can then be used to stuff a turkey or chicken. Just be sure to allow the mixture to cool completely before stuffing the cavity of the bird. Or, if you wish, the mixture can be served as a casserole. Grease a casserole or baking dish with the melted butter, add the dressing, and bake at 350°F until warmed through, 15 to 20 minutes.

When Eula Mae was a young child, times were hard. It was during the Depression, but because they lived on a farm, there was always food. It may have been plain, but it was nourishing. They always had the ingredients to make cornbread and butter and syrup to put on it.

"When I was growing up, we lived on cornbread. We had it buttered and drizzled with pure cane syrup for breakfast, but we also ate it with other meals. It was kind of like sliced bread for us. It's great for mopping up gravy or sopping up the juices in the vegetable pot. We must not waste! And, darling, cornbread can be used to make tasty dressings as well."

Country Cornbread

MAKES 6 TO 8 SERVINGS

2 tablespoons vegetable oil

1 cup yellow cornmeal

$^3/_4$ cup all-purpose flour

1 teaspoon salt

$1^1/_2$ teaspoons baking powder

$1^1/_2$ cups buttermilk

$^1/_2$ teaspoon baking soda

1 large egg

$^1/_4$ cup ($^1/_2$ stick) butter, melted, at room temperature

1. Preheat the oven to 475°F. Put the oil in an 8- or 9-inch heavy, ovenproof skillet (preferably cast iron) and set in the oven to heat for about 5 minutes.

2. Combine the cornmeal, flour, salt, baking powder, and buttermilk in a large mixing bowl and stir to blend. Stir in the baking soda.

3. Combine the egg and melted butter in a small bowl and whisk to blend. Add to the cornbread batter and stir to blend.

4. Remove the skillet from the oven and pour in the cornbread batter. Bake until golden brown, about 20 minutes. Remove from the oven. Cut into wedges to serve.

NOTE If the cornbread is to be used as the basis for a dressing, let cool completely and follow the recipe directions.

Because Eula Mae's father was a farmer, they cooked with whatever they grew, raised, or came by from their neighbors. But there were always sugar and sweet potatoes.

"Papa often had a sack of raw sugar from the sugar mill after the sugarcane harvest. Sometimes we sprinkled some of the sugar on oatmeal or sweet potatoes. Some of it, though, was used for this wonderful dish of sweet potatoes. This recipe is as old as I am!"

Raw sugar is sugar before it's refined; it's coarse and brown, with a molasses flavor, and is available in many supermarkets. If you can't find it, you can substitute refined sugar, but the taste will be different.

SWEET POTATOES ROLLED IN RAW SUGAR

MAKES 8 SERVINGS

8 medium-size sweet potatoes
1 cup raw or unrefined sugar
1 teaspoon ground cinnamon
$^1/_4$ teaspoon ground mace
1 cup fresh orange juice
$^1/_4$ cup ($^1/_2$ stick) butter, cut into bits

1. Preheat the oven to 300°F.

2. Line a baking sheet with parchment paper or aluminum foil and arrange the sweet potatoes on it. Bake until tender, about 1 hour. Remove from the oven, let cool, and peel.

3. Increase the oven temperature to 350°F.

4. Combine the sugar, cinnamon, and mace in a large shallow dish. Roll each potato in the mixture to coat evenly.

5. Pour the orange juice into a baking dish. Arrange the potatoes in the dish in a single layer and scatter the butter bits evenly over the top of the potatoes. Bake for 30 minutes. Remove from the oven and baste the potatoes with the pan juices. Serve warm.

Eula Mae has the talent of taking the simplest ingredients and turning them into something delicious. Carrots lightly flavored with mint and cream are a delightful side dish for a holiday meal.

"I like the bright color of carrots, don't you? And they're always available at the supermarkets."

MINTED CARROTS WITH CREAM

MAKES 6 SERVINGS

6 medium-size carrots, scraped and cut crosswise into $^1/_2$-inch-thick slices
$^1/_4$ cup ($^1/_2$ stick) butter
1 tablespoon firmly packed light brown sugar
1 tablespoon granulated sugar
$^1/_4$ cup heavy cream
1 tablespoon chopped fresh mint leaves

1. Drop the carrots in boiling water and cook at a boil until just tender, about 15 minutes. Remove from the heat and drain. Set aside.

2. Combine the butter, brown sugar, granulated sugar, heavy cream, and mint in a medium-size saucepan over medium heat. Stir to dissolve the sugars and cook, stirring occasionally, until the mixture thickens slightly, 6 to 8 minutes. Add the carrots and heat for several minutes. Serve warm.

Bread pudding is very popular in this area of the country. You know why? No one ever lets anything go to waste. When there is day-old or stale bread, this is the ideal dish to make. Most of the time, Eula Mae's bread pudding is made with bread, eggs, sugar, and milk.

"But I heard someone talk about a bread pudding made with chocolate and, you know me, I had to try it. It quickly became a favorite of mine. Susan, my daughter, loves this. MoNeg favored the traditional one. Everyone is different."

Eula Mae does not have all kinds of modern kitchen equipment or gadgets, but she has a small microwave.

"Well, sometimes modern conveniences come in handy, I admit. I use it to melt the butter and chocolate for this pudding, but you can do it in a small sauce-pan on the stove over low heat."

CHOCOLATE BREAD PUDDING

MAKES ABOUT 10 SERVINGS

4 ounces unsweetened chocolate

$1/4$ cup ($1/2$ stick) butter

6 cups cubed bread, crusts removed

1 quart milk

6 large eggs, separated

$1^3/4$ cups sugar

$1^1/2$ teaspoons pure vanilla extract

$1/4$ teaspoon cream of tartar

1. Preheat the oven to 325°F. Lightly grease a 12 x 8 x 2-inch baking dish.

2. Microwave the chocolate and butter together in a large microwave-safe bowl on high until soft and melted, about 2 minutes. Stir to blend.

3. Combine the bread and milk in a large mixing bowl and let stand for 10 to 15 minutes.

4. Combine the egg yolks, 1 cup of the sugar, and the vanilla together in another large mixing bowl and beat with an electric mixer on high speed until the mixture is light colored. Beat in the chocolate mixture, then gradually stir into the bread mixture. Pour into the prepared baking dish. Bake until the mixture sets, 35 to 45 minutes. Wash and dry the mixer beaters well.

5. Remove the pudding from the oven and increase the oven temperature to 375°F.

6. Beat the egg whites in a large mixing bowl with the electric mixer on high speed until foamy. Gradually beat in the remaining ¾ cup sugar and the cream of tartar. Continue beating until stiff peaks form. Spread the meringue evenly on top of the pudding. Bake until lightly browned, 12 to 15 minutes. Serve warm.

"Susan, my daughter, loves this cake and said it had to go in this book. I fix it often and I must say, it is unlike anything I've ever eaten. It's an old recipe, but *chère*, it is very good. I only wish I could have real, homemade butter like we had at our farm. It would make the cake even better," says Eula Mae. "It is a very special recipe and ideal for a Thanksgiving dessert. It is very important to cut the pecans evenly and finely. Don't grind them in a food processor. It just isn't the same."

OLD-FASHIONED NUT CAKE

MAKES 1 CAKE; SERVES 12 TO 14

1 pound (4 sticks) plus 2 tablespoons butter

2 cups plus 1 tablespoon sugar

2 cups all-purpose flour

2 teaspoons unsweetened cocoa powder

$1/4$ teaspoon salt

4 large eggs

1 teaspoon pure vanilla extract

4 cups finely chopped pecans

1. Preheat the oven to 300°F. Butter a Bundt or tube pan or a large loaf pan with the 2 tablespoons butter. Sprinkle the pan evenly with the 1 tablespoon sugar. Set aside.

2. Put the pound of butter in a large mixing bowl. Cut the sticks into small pieces and let them sit until they come to room temperature and are very soft.

3. Sift the flour, cocoa, and salt into a medium-size mixing bowl. Set aside.

4. By hand and with a good sturdy spoon (not with an electric mixer), beat the eggs in a large mixing bowl. Add the sugar a little (about 2 tablespoons) at a time and blend after each addition. (You want the mixture to be creamy and fluffy.) Stir in the vanilla and softened butter. Add the sifted flour mixture. Stir in one direction until well mixed. Add the pecans and mix well.

5. Scrape the batter into the prepared pan and bake until golden brown, about 1 hour. Remove from the oven and let cool for a few minutes in the pan. Turn the cake out of its pan onto a wire rack and cool completely before slicing to serve.

PAUL GOES HUNTING

Deep Bayou Punch

Mr. Paul's Wild Duck Salad

Ti Bruce's Duck Gumbo

Tarte à la Bouillie

With the first hint of cool weather in September, the egrets and other species of birds that have spent the spring and summer on Avery Island leave for the long flight south over the Gulf of Mexico to warmer winter weather.

Waterfowl, probably millions, come from the north in autumn and stay the winter. The marshland around the Island is a haven for migrating birds and most men, and a few women, spend most weekends at private camps or lodges along the southern coast of the state hoping to bag their limit.

The weeks before hunting season begins, the hunters spend hours building blinds—camouflaged platforms—where they sit, huddled against the cold, to wait for the great flocks of mallards, pintails, ring-necked ducks, and Canada geese that migrate during this time of year. The hunters will get up before dawn to be sure they're in their blinds waiting for the sun to rise, which is when the waterfowl begin flying into marshes, ponds, bayous, and other waterways along the Gulf Coast.

Not far from the Island is the Rockefeller Wildlife Refuge, about 84,000 acres in all, which borders the Gulf of Mexico and where hundreds of thousands of waterfowl and marsh birds—geese, ducks, coots, gallinules, and rails—find a winter sanctuary. It is here that the official state bird, the brown pelican, soars gracefully over the flat marshland and the trembling prairies (called *prairie tremblante* by the Acadians, this is a vast area of aquatic grasses and reeds). The refuge is also the home of thousands of alligators, otters, raccoons, muskrats, nutria, and deer.

Paul McIlhenny grew up in New Orleans, spending a good deal of time on the Island. He is an avid hunter and loves to have guests join him in a hunt or two. Afterward, of course, he hosts a feast that features what bounty they have bagged.

"I never know what Mr. Paul is going to bring me to cook. Sometimes there are several mallards and teals, and other times there might be a few geese, all of which can be made into a gumbo or jambalaya, or roasted long and slow. The preparation of these dishes is easy when you have such good ingredients," says Eula Mae.

The refuge is also the home of thousands of alligators, otters, raccoons, muskrats, nutria, and deer.

Eula Mae found this recipe in her husband's file box. At the bottom of the paper on which it is written, it says, "Do not drink this before going hunting!"

As you can see, the ingredients are mighty powerful, so you had best drink it when you come back from hunting. If some hunters' accounts of what goes on at the camp after the hunt can be believed, most of the pleasure is the camaraderie enjoyed at the end of the day.

Eula Mae told me that she knows why men love to congregate at their camps and lodges.

"The men like to relax, have a few drinks, cook a gumbo or roast a few ducks. A lot of the men in south Louisiana are great cooks because they are not uneasy about working in a kitchen. MoNeg loved going on the hunt, having a few laughs with his friends, having a nip, and, of course, cooking a big meal. Lots of men are very proud, and well they should be, of their know-how in the kitchen."

DEEP BAYOU PUNCH

MAKES ABOUT 2 1/2 QUARTS

6 oranges

4 lemons

4 tea bags

2 gallons water

Sugar to taste

1 fifth orange wine (recipe follows)

1 quart whiskey

1. Cut the oranges and lemons in half. Place them, the tea bags, and water in a large pot, bring to a boil, and let boil until the rinds of the citrus are soft.

2. Strain the liquid and sweeten with sugar to taste. Add the wine and whiskey to the hot liquid and serve immediately.

Orange Wine

2 cups white rum

Juice and rinds of 10 oranges

1 cup sugar

3 cinnamon sticks

2 cloves

5 allspice berries

Pinch of ground anise

1 tablespoon pure vanilla extract

1 tablespoon ground nutmeg

1. Combine all the ingredients in a large glass jar. Cover the jar and let the mixture sit for 2 days. The jar should be shaken several times during the 2 days.

2. Strain through a colander or sieve. Refrigerate until ready to serve.

"**I**'ve been making this duck salad for wild game neophytes and it's always enjoyed," says Paul McIlhenny. "And what's great about it is that it's really two meals in one. The broth from the duck can be served hot with buckwheat noodles and, of course, you have the salad to accompany it."

He showed Eula Mae how to prepare it and she continues to make it for Mr. Paul, with her usual TLC, whenever he shows up with some ducks.

MR. PAUL'S WILD DUCK SALAD

MAKES ABOUT 6 SERVINGS

FOR THE DUCKS

2 mallard ducks, cleaned and rinsed under cool water

1 large yellow onion, coarsely chopped

3 ribs celery, chopped

1 medium-size bell pepper, seeded and chopped

2 to 3 sprigs fresh parsley

3 bay leaves

2 teaspoons salt

1 teaspoon freshly ground black pepper

FOR THE SALAD

1 cup mayonnaise, or more as needed

$^2/_3$ cup chopped green onions (green and white parts)

$^2/_3$ cup chopped celery

1 tablespoon Major Grey's chutney, chopped

$^1/_2$ teaspoon Tabasco brand pepper sauce

$^1/_2$ teaspoon freshly ground black pepper

1. To prepare the ducks, put them in a large, heavy pot or Dutch oven and cover with water. Add the onion, celery, bell pepper, parsley, bay leaves, salt, and pepper. Bring to a boil, then reduce the heat to medium-low and simmer, partially covered, until the ducks are very tender, about 2 hours.

2. Remove from the heat and strain through a fine-mesh sieve. Reserve the broth. When the meat is cool enough to handle, remove it from the bones, discarding any fat or skin, and chop into bite-size chunks.

3. To prepare the salad, in a large mixing bowl, combine the duck meat, mayonnaise, green onions, celery, chutney, Tabasco, and black pepper. Add more mayonnaise and salt according to taste. Chill for about 30 minutes before serving.

The salad can be served on a bed of greens. The broth can be reheated before serving.

When Mr. Walter McIlhenny had his boat, *The Heron*, his cook onboard was Emery Broussard, nicknamed "Ti Bruce." Mr. Walter loved to entertain on the boat and it was nothing to bring along a pot of gumbo made with ducks that were bagged on a hunt.

"You know, they had fun," says Eula Mae. "Ah, the men would get so excited, getting the boat ready and stocked. I can see them even now, the boat engine idling while they filled ice chests with soft drinks, beer, wine, and, of course, the food. Then, off they would go, down Bayou Petite Anse heading out to Vermilion Bay for a day or evening on the water!"

Here is a duck gumbo similar to one Ti Bruce often prepared for the men when they went hunting and fishing. It's best to use wild duck, but you can substitute farm-raised.

TI BRUCE'S DUCK GUMBO

MAKES 4 TO 6 SERVINGS

2 mallards or 4 teals (4 to 5 pounds total), cleaned and rinsed under cool water

1 teaspoon Tabasco brand pepper sauce

1 teaspoon salt

2 tablespoons vegetable oil

2 tablespoons butter

3 tablespoons all-purpose flour

1 cup chopped yellow onions

1 cup seeded and chopped green bell peppers

1/2 cup chopped celery

2 garlic cloves, chopped

3 cups chicken broth

2 dozen shucked oysters (optional)

1/4 cup chopped green onions (green and white parts)

1/4 cup chopped fresh parsley leaves

Hot cooked long-grain white rice (see page 171)

1. Season the ducks with ½ teaspoon of the Tabasco and the salt. Heat the oil in large, deep pot or Dutch oven over medium-high heat. Add the ducks and brown on all sides. Remove and set aside. Pour off the fat.

2. Melt the butter in the same pot over medium-high heat. Stir in the flour and cook, stirring constantly, to make a chocolate brown roux (see Eula Mae's advice on making a roux, page 94). Add the onions, bell peppers, celery, and garlic and cook, stirring often, until soft, about 5 minutes. Gradually add the broth and the remaining ½ teaspoon Tabasco. Cook until slightly thickened, about 5 minutes.

3. Return the ducks to the pot and bring to a boil. Cover, reduce the heat to medium-low, and simmer until the duck is tender, about 1 hour.

4. Add the oysters, if you wish, the green onions, and parsley. Cook until the oysters curl, about 8 minutes. Adjust the seasonings if necessary. Serve hot over the rice.

gain, this is one of those dishes that represents the type of cooking the Cajuns developed. The ingredients are simple—milk, eggs, butter—all available on the farms where they lived. It is, and was, a cuisine of "making do" with what's at hand.

Tarte à la bouillie (loosely translated, it means a tart or pie filled with boiled custard) is a south Louisiana thing. Anybody over the age of, say, fifty years old who lives in this area will tell you, "Oh, yes, my grandmother and old aunts used to make them."

"Well!" Eula Mae exclaims. "I've been making them practically all my life! The custard is rich and creamy, and I usually make extra custard because everyone who comes through the kitchen while it's cooking wants a spoon or two. I remember one fellow who visited the Island asking for a bowl of the pudding. He wasn't interested in the pie; he wanted just the pudding! That made me happy!"

TARTE À LA BOUILLIE

MAKES 1 PIE; SERVES 6

1 quart plus $^{1}/_{4}$ cup milk

2 large egg yolks

2 cups sugar

One 13-ounce can evaporated milk

2 teaspoons pure vanilla extract

2 $^{3}/_{4}$ cups plus 2 tablespoons all-purpose flour

$^{1}/_{2}$ cup (1 stick) butter, softened

1 teaspoon baking powder

1. Place 1 quart of the milk in a heavy Dutch oven and heat over medium heat until bubbles begin to form all around the edge of the pot. Do not let it come to a boil. Set aside.

2. Using an electric mixer, beat the egg yolks until thick and lemon colored on low speed. Add 1 cup of the sugar and beat well. Add the evaporated milk and 1 teaspoon of the vanilla, mixing well on low speed with the mixer. Stir in $^{3}/_{4}$ cup of the flour. Gradually stir in about $^{1}/_{4}$ of the hot milk into the egg mixture. Add this mixture back into the remaining hot milk, stirring constantly. Cook over medium heat, stirring constantly, until thick and smooth, about

15 minutes. Gently stir in 4 tablespoons (½ stick) of the butter and remove from the heat. Set aside to cool completely.

3. Cream the remaining 4 tablespoons (½ stick) butter in a large mixing bowl, gradually adding the remaining 1 cup sugar, beating well. Add 2 cups of the flour and the baking powder, beating on low speed with the mixer until the mixture resembles coarse meal. Add the remaining ¼ cup milk and 1 teaspoon vanilla, stirring until well blended. The dough will be crumbly at first but will form a smooth ball with continued mixing. Turn the dough out onto a work surface and knead 4 or 5 times. Divide the dough in half.

4. Preheat the oven to 350°F.

5. Sprinkle the remaining 2 tablespoons flour on waxed paper. Press one portion of the dough into a 14-inch circle. Carefully transfer the pastry (floured side down) to a buttered 9-inch deep-dish pie pan. Fill the pastry shell with the custard, reserving 1¼ cups. Place the other portion of dough on waxed paper and press into an 11-inch circle. Carefully place the pastry over the filling. Do not slit the top crust. Seal and flute the edges together. Bake until lightly browned, about 35 minutes. Remove the pie from the oven and let cool to room temperature before serving.

6. Spoon the reserved custard into individual serving dishes, chill, and serve at another time.

WINTER

Winter in the Deep South is relatively mild, though the temperature can dip below freezing from time to time and on occasion it has even snowed. But because it's so damp, the cold is bone chilling. The landscape for the most part is gray and foreboding. Save for the leaves on the live oaks and some evergreens, the countryside can be bleak, but it is appealing in its own fashion. The stark, leafless cypress

trees draped with Spanish moss on the Island stand like sentinels on the edges of the bayous and waterways. The sunsets, now earlier in the afternoon, are more majestic, or so it seems, since there is less foliage to obstruct the view. And then there are times when a thick fog, almost blue in color, rolls in from the bays, shrouding the monotonous flatness of the land.

"When I was a young girl, winter was a time when I could take it a bit easier. All the crops were in and the garden vegetables were just about finished, save for some mustard greens and turnips. I couldn't do much to prepare for holiday meals in advance because we didn't have modern refrigeration. But there were still all the farm chores—milking the cows, making butter, feeding the chickens—to be done, even when it was cold."

After Eula Mae married and moved to the Island, she and MoNeg were kept busy year-round at the Commissary.

"We had our routine. Up early in the morning, filled orders, took inventory, prepared for lunch service, and cooked our evening meals."

"I don't mind wintertime," said Eula Mae one day, as she sipped a cup of coffee. "I like to go through the different seasons because each time of year has its good things. For instance, when we have a cold front blow in from the west, it's a good time to make gumbo. Sometimes I make chicken and sausage gumbo; other times I like one made with local seafood. The aroma of those thick soups simmering makes me feel good all over.

"The holidays are always a special time and a busy one for me. I like being in my kitchen making holidays treats, having my daughter and her family for dinner, and helping the other families on the Island prepare their feasts. There are always lots of visitors, so we have to cook lots of food!"

In between the cold fronts that bring rain and chilly winds, there are some downright pleasant days, some as balmy as those in early spring. But whatever the weather brings, activities continue rolling right along. After the holidays of Christmas and New Year's, Carnival season begins on January 6, known locally as Twelfth Night. The carnival season runs at full throttle with parties, parades, ball, dinners, and brunches until Mardi Gras Day, or Shrove Tuesday.

CHRISTMAS SUPPER AT THE TANGO

Peppered Pork Roast

Eggplant Dressing

My Macaroni and Cheese

Sweet Potato Pone

Susan's Rum Cake

Divinity Fudge

Eula Mae's Pralines

Peanut Brittle

"The Christmas holidays of my childhood were simple. We didn't have much money for toys, so we made some of our own. We made dolls out of old socks and stuffed them with moss. The boys made holes in large tin cans and secured twine in the holes. Then we could stand on the cans, hold the twine in our hands, and "walk" around. We loved that because it made us taller!" Eula Mae says with a laugh. "Of course, we ate what we had on the farm. We might have had some fine roasting chickens and some of our canned vegetables that we put up. And I made lots of fresh bread and pies. *Chère*, we always had plenty to eat. It was simple but always good."

When Eula Mae and her husband came to live on the Island, she continued most of her holiday traditions, and MoNeg started one of his.

"Just about every year on Christmas Eve, MoNeg dragged out a homemade smoker he had made out of an old oil barrel. He cleaned it and got it ready to smoke whatever meats he had chosen. Sometimes it was a pork roast, other times it might have been some mallards or pintails that his hunting friends had given him. He seasoned his pork or birds just right, with lots of pepper and salt and only he knew what else! He gathered some pecan wood because he said that made the best 'smoking' wood. It burned slowly and didn't give off too much smoke. Then, before we left for Midnight Mass at the church near the Island, he would put the roast or birds in the smoker. When we returned home, he would check, add more wood, and let it smoke through the night. By morning, everything was cooked to perfection. Ah, he was a smart man and a good cook."

The meal was usually eaten in early afternoon, and friends on the Island would come by to visit later in the day.

And, of course, the McIlhenny clan descends, *en masse*, upon the Island for the Christmas holidays. Christmas is indeed a grand occasion on the Island. Many members of the McIlhenny clan, and their guests, gather at their homes for a week or two of respite from their busy lives. There might be an impromptu cocktail party at Marsh House, a rambling home that is ideal for holiday functions. With huge fireplaces, spacious rooms, and a totally equipped kitchen, Marsh House is often filled with people relaxing, enjoying the vistas of the Island, and, of course, consuming drink and food.

Eula Mae is very familiar with these gatherings.

"I love nothing better than preparing delicacies for the parties at Marsh House because everyone enjoys them. The family members and the guests are in and out of the large kitchen, sampling this, tasting that!

"But I always give myself some meditation moments to think about all that has happened in the past year. I try to remember all the special events, or a simple thing like having one of the children come by the house to say hello, or taking my grandchildren for a walk through the woods, pointing out a deer or a rabbit."

Eula Mae is also busy making gifts for family and friends.

"Gifts can be as simple as a box of homemade fudge or peanut brittle. It's not necessarily the gift itself that makes it special, but the time and effort that it takes to make it. It's the idea of giving that makes this time of year so dear to me. And, of course, sitting down at the holiday table with all of my family to enjoy good food is the highlight of the season."

The best cut for this pork roast is what is locally called a fresh ham shank.

"My husband often seasoned and stuffed the roast the day before Christmas and cooked it long and slow in a large oven at the Commissary for hours. The skin was crispy and tender like a potato chip," recalls Eula Mae.

It is a popular dish throughout south Louisiana, and the aroma of the roast baking wafts through the air early on holiday mornings. The taste, with the onions, peppers, and garlic stuffed in the roast, is mouthwatering.

PEPPERED PORK ROAST

MAKES 12 TO 14 SERVINGS

1 fresh ham shank (10 to 12 pounds)
1 cup finely chopped yellow onions
$1/2$ cup seeded and finely chopped green bell peppers
6 to 8 garlic cloves, thinly sliced
4 teaspoons salt
4 teaspoons cayenne
1 teaspoon freshly ground black pepper
1 teaspoon Tabasco brand pepper sauce
3 tablespoons vegetable oil
2 to 3 cups water, as needed

1. Preheat the oven to 450°F.

2. Place the ham on a large cutting board or a clean dish towel on a work surface. Combine the onions, bell peppers, garlic, 3 teaspoons of the salt, and 3 teaspoons of the cayenne, the black pepper, and Tabasco in a medium-size mixing bowl. With a sharp, thin knife, make several deep slits in the roast spaced several inches apart. Stuff 2 to 3 tablespoons of the seasoning mixture into each hole, pressing it in firmly with your fingers. Rub the outside of the roast with the vegetable oil, then rub it with the remaining 1 teaspoon each salt and cayenne.

3. Place the meat in a large roasting pan and roast until it browns evenly, 30 to 40 minutes. When the bottom of the pan begins to sizzle, add 2 cups of the water. Reduce the oven

temperature to 350°F. Cover and continue to roast, adding more water to the pan if it becomes dry, until the ham is very tender and the juices run clear, 3 to 4 hours. Baste occasionally with the pan juices.

4. Remove the roast from the oven and let sit for 15 minutes to settle the juices before carving to serve. Be sure to serve with the pan juices; they're dark and thick and delicious.

Because eggplant is grown in home gardens during the summer, it is smothered and put up in the freezer to be used as the basis of dishes like this one during the colder months. "Smothering" is a very typical procedure for many dishes in south Louisiana. For instance, there is the wonderful dish called crawfish étouffée. *Étouffer* simply means "to smother" and in cooking it has another translation and that is "to smother in its own juices." Onions, bell peppers, and celery, the vegetables that are used in many traditional south Louisiana dishes, are cooked in butter or oil, after which one can add other vegetables (eggplant, in this case), or crawfish, or shrimp, and the mixture is cooked until it has absorbed all the flavors.

"Ah, yes, smothering vegetables and some seafoods gives whatever you're cooking a very intense flavor," explains Eula Mae.

This dish is similar to rice dressing, but without the giblets and a roux.

"I like dressings made with local vegetables and this one has been on my Christmas menu for most of my life. It has a sweetness to it, and it goes well with poultry, beef, or pork. Make it a day ahead and store it in the refrigerator."

EGGPLANT DRESSING

MAKES 8 TO 10 SERVINGS

1 tablespoon vegetable oil

1 pound ground beef

1 pound ground pork

1 cup chopped yellow onions

1 cup seeded and chopped green bell peppers

$1/2$ cup chopped celery

3 garlic cloves, peeled

2 medium-size eggplants, peeled and cubed

$1/2$ teaspoon salt

$1/4$ teaspoon freshly ground black pepper

$1/4$ teaspoon Tabasco brand pepper sauce

2 cups hot cooked long-grain white rice (see box)

1. In a large, heavy saucepan, heat the oil over medium heat. Add the ground beef and pork and cook, stirring often, until all pink has disappeared, about 15 minutes. Add the onions, bell peppers, celery, and garlic and cook, stirring often, until soft, about 5 minutes. Add the eggplant, salt, black pepper, and Tabasco and stir to mix. Cover the pot and cook, stirring occasionally, until the eggplant is very soft and tender, about 30 minutes.

2. Add the rice and mix well. Add more salt and pepper, if you wish. Serve warm.

Eula Mae's Method for Cooking Rice

For each cup of uncooked rice (1 cup raw = 3 cups cooked), add 2 cups cold water to a saucepan with 1 teaspoon salt, 1 teaspoon distilled white vinegar, and 1 tablespoon butter. All this goes in at once. Cover and bring to a boil, then reduce the heat to medium-low and cook until all liquid evaporates and the rice is tender, 20 to 30 minutes.

Homemade macaroni and cheese is almost as popular as rice and gravy in rural south Louisiana. It is always included as a side dish for holidays and celebrations.

"If I didn't have macaroni and cheese for Christmas dinner, I don't know what my family would say. And don't let me catch you making macaroni and cheese out of the box! It just isn't the same as homemade, made with that TLC that I always talk about!"

MY MACARONI AND CHEESE

MAKES 6 SERVINGS

2 quarts water

1 tablespoon olive oil

1 tablespoon salt

$1/2$ pound elbow macaroni

$1/4$ cup ($1/2$ stick) butter

$1/4$ cup finely chopped yellow onions

3 tablespoons all-purpose flour

$1/4$ teaspoon Tabasco brand pepper sauce

$1^1/2$ cups half-and-half

2 cups grated American or Cheddar cheese

1. Preheat the oven to 350°F. Lightly oil a large baking dish.

2. Combine the water, olive oil, and salt in a large saucepan and bring to a boil over medium-high heat. Add the macaroni, reduce the heat to medium, cover, and cook until tender, 8 to 10 minutes. Drain and rinse under cold running water. Set aside. Dry the saucepan.

3. In the same saucepan, melt the butter over medium heat. Add the onions and cook, stirring, until just soft, about 3 minutes. Add the flour and Tabasco sauce and whisk to blend. Slowly add the half-and-half, whisking constantly, until the mixture thickens. Add the cheese and stir until completely melted and the mixture is thick and smooth.

4. Add the macaroni and toss to coat evenly. Pour the mixture into the prepared baking dish. Cover lightly with aluminum foil and bake until bubbly, about 20 minutes. Remove from the oven and serve warm.

A popular dish in the South is corn pone, which is an eggless cornbread shaped into small ovals that are either fried or baked. This dish, made with sweet potatoes, is also a type of pone. It is made with freshly grated sweet potatoes and has long been a favorite on the Island.

"*Chère*, I prefer using a hand grater rather than a food processor. Grating them in a food processor makes them too watery. You really can see the difference. Grate some of the potatoes finely and some coarsely to give it a nice texture. You might want to soak the grated sweet potatoes in cool water to keep them crisp and retain the bright color. This dish has creamy butter and fresh eggs that make it so rich that some claim they could eat it for dessert!

"And, *chère*, beat the eggs until they are foamy and beat the sugar and butter together well for a good texture."

SWEET POTATO PONE

MAKES 12 SERVINGS

1 cup sugar

$1/4$ cup ($1/2$ stick) butter, at room temperature

2 large eggs, well beaten until foamy

1 cup Steen's 100% Pure Cane Syrup

One 12-ounce can evaporated milk

$1/2$ teaspoon ground nutmeg

$1/2$ teaspoon ground cinnamon

3 cups peeled and finely grated sweet potatoes

1 cup peeled and coarsely grated sweet potatoes

1 teaspoon grated orange zest

1 teaspoon grated lemon zest

$1/4$ cup all-purpose flour

1. Preheat the oven to 350°F. Lightly oil the bottom and sides of a 9 x 13-inch baking pan.

2. Combine the sugar and the butter in a medium-size mixing bowl and cream well with the back of a large wooden spoon until well blended. Add the eggs and whisk to blend well. Add the cane syrup and mix well. Add the evaporated milk, nutmeg, and cinnamon and stir well to blend. Add the sweet potatoes and orange and lemon zest and mix well again. Add the flour and stir only in one direction to blend. Pour the mixture into the prepared pan.

3. Bake until the center sets and a toothpick inserted into the center comes out clean, about 1½ hours. Remove from the oven and let sit about 5 minutes. Cut into squares to serve.

Baba (bah-bah), also known as *baba au rhum*, is a cake traditionally made with raisins and soaked in rum. It appeared often on the menus in old New Orleans restaurants, but it's no longer around. Susan, Eula Mae's daughter, has created her own version.

"Susan has been making this cake for years for Christmas. She made it for her neighbors when she and her husband moved into their new home. It was a way to get to know them and give them something for the holidays. She wraps the cake in pretty Christmas wrap and ties a big bow on the package," says Eula Mae.

Susan has a story of her own.

"My next door neighbor and I had a good laugh one year. I usually deliver the cakes on Christmas Eve and her daughter refused to eat breakfast until the cake arrived. I was very complimented that the cake had become such a treat for her," recalls Susan. "I think you'll find this to be the perfect dessert after a holiday meal because it's festive and rich."

SUSAN'S RUM CAKE

MAKES 1 BUNDT CAKE; SERVES 10 TO 12

1 cup chopped pecans
One 18¼-ounce box yellow cake mix
One 3-ounce package instant vanilla pudding
¾ cup water
½ cup vegetable oil
¼ cup dark rum
4 large eggs
1 recipe Rum Sauce (recipe follows)

1. Preheat the oven to 325°F. Lightly coat the inside of a Bundt pan with nonstick cooking spray. Sprinkle the pecans evenly on the bottom of the pan. Set aside.

2. Combine the cake mix, pudding mix, water, oil, and rum in a large mixing bowl. Stir to blend. Add the eggs one at a time, beating in between each addition. Pour the batter into the prepared pan and bake until the cake is lightly browned and a toothpick inserted in the center comes out clean, about 1 hour.

3. Remove the cake from the oven and poke holes all over the top of the cake with the tines of a fork. Pour the sauce evenly over the top of the cake. Let cool completely in the pan. Remove the cake from the pan and slice to serve.

Rum Sauce

MAKES ABOUT ³/₄ CUP

¹/₂ **cup (1 stick) butter**
¹/₃ **cup sugar**
¹/₄ **cup water**
1 tablespoon dark rum
1 teaspoon pure vanilla extract

Bring the butter, sugar, water, and rum to a boil in a small saucepan. Cook, stirring, until the sugar dissolves, 3 to 4 minutes. Remove from the heat and stir in the vanilla. Let cool a bit before pouring over the cake.

Divinity fudge is a favorite candy to make during the holidays in south Louisiana. Some cooks like to add a couple of drops of red or green food coloring to the candy in the final step to give it a festive color.

When Eula Mae told me she was going to show me how to make divinity fudge, I couldn't wait. But wait I did, because she told me the weather had to be dry and cold if we were to succeed.

"You see, if the weather is hot and damp, the candy will not set up properly, or it will take forever. It's best that there is no moisture in the air. The same rule holds true when making pralines and other candies," explained Eula Mae.

"Always chop your pecans nicely because you want them to be pretty in your fudge. I use an old cherry jar that I've had for years to measure my ingredients. I fill the jar almost all the way to the top with corn syrup, then I add enough water to completely fill the jar. When toasting the pecans I know they're done when I smell them.

And don't forget, take your time. You can't make this fudge in a hurry!

DIVINITY FUDGE

MAKES ABOUT 16 PIECES

3 tablespoons butter

2 cups chopped pecans

2 large egg whites

2 cups sugar

$1/3$ cup light corn syrup

$1/4$ cup water

1. Preheat the oven to 250°F. Grease an 8 x 12-inch baking dish with the butter. Set aside.

2. Arrange the pecan pieces evenly on a baking sheet. Bake until brown and toasted, about 15 minutes. Remove from the oven and set aside to cool.

3. In a large mixing bowl, beat the egg whites with an electric mixer until stiff. Set aside.

4. Combine the sugar, corn syrup, and water in a heavy, deep saucepan over medium-low heat. Stir until the sugar dissolves. Continue stirring and cooking until the soft-crack stage, 270° to 290°F on a candy thermometer (see page 15), about 20 minutes.

5. With the electric mixer on medium-high speed, slowly, slowly add the hot mixture to the egg whites, beating constantly until the mixture turns glossy. Add the pecans and mix well with a wooden spoon, then pour into the prepared dish.

6. Let sit until cooled completely, about 45 minutes. Cut into squares.

Pralines are a sugary concoction and much favored during the Christmas holidays. Again, it's best to make pralines when the weather is cold and dry, as dampness will delay (or prevent) the candy from setting.

"I always preferred pralines to cookies during the holidays, and always had the ingredients on hand for when the weather was ideal for making them. Pralines should be rich and creamy, as far as I'm concerned, although some people like them crunchy. I always made several batches of pralines to offer to guests or to give as gifts. Around here we always have something good and sweet around to serve with coffee during the day or after the holiday meal. Don't stress yourself out, take your time. Oh, and be sure you pick over the pecans so there aren't any shells. And, *chère*, be sure and toast your pecans before adding them to the candy.

"Before you begin, put several layers of old newspaper on your countertop. Then top with a single layer of waxed paper. Of course, if you have a slab of marble, that's wonderful. I have a small slab, but it's so heavy I don't use it as much as I used to. If you don't have a horse, ride the mule, my father used to say."

Use small pecan halves. If all you have is large, cut them in half.

EULA MAE'S PRALINES

MAKES ABOUT 2 DOZEN

$4^{1}/_{3}$ cups pecan halves

One 12-ounce can evaporated milk

1 cup heavy cream

4 cups sugar

2 tablespoons light corn syrup

1 teaspoon pure vanilla extract

2 tablespoons butter, at room temperature

1. Preheat the oven to 250°F. Put the pecans in a shallow baking pan or rimmed cookie sheet in a single layer. Bake until aromatic, about 15 minutes. Remove from the oven, stir, and let cool. Set aside.

2. Combine the evaporated milk, heavy cream, and sugar in a large, heavy saucepan over medium heat and stir to mix. Cook, stirring often, until the sugar is completely dissolved. Continue to cook, stirring often, until it comes to a boil. Add the corn syrup and stir constantly (stay with it—and keep stirring to prevent it boiling over) until it reaches the soft-ball stage, about 240°F on a candy thermometer (see page 15). It will take 35 to 45 minutes, depending on the weather.

3. Add the pecans and stir to mix. Continue to stir over medium heat until the mixture returns to a rolling boil. It will thicken and, as you stir, you will see a film of sugar begin to form on the inside of the pot as it reaches the soft-ball stage again. (Eula Mae has her own rule about when the syrup is ready—when you lift the spoon and two drops meet as they drip off the bowl of the spoon.) Remove from the heat.

4. Add the vanilla and butter and stir to mix. Continue to stir until the mixture becomes thick and creamy, and sugary around the edge of the mixture, about 15 minutes. The mixture will be a taffy color.

5. Working quickly, spoon the mixture, about a heaping kitchen spoon at a time, onto the waxed paper. Let cool completely before lifting off with a thin-bladed knife. The pralines can be stored between layers of waxed paper in an airtight container for up to 1 week.

Many farmers in Louisiana raised peanuts in their home gardens because of their many uses and nutritional value. They were boiled or roasted, and used to make this brittle for the holidays.

"My father loved peanut brittle and I made it often for him when I was a young girl. We made this brittle simply because we had all the ingredients available on the farm. I continue to make this to give as gifts and to have for the family."

It can be stored in an airtight container for several days. It is also sensitive to the weather, so be sure you make it on a cold, dry day.

PEANUT BRITTLE

MAKES ABOUT 1 ^{1}/$_2$ POUNDS

2 cups sugar
^{1}/$_2$ cup light corn syrup
2 cups raw shelled peanuts
1 teaspoon baking soda
Pinch of salt

1. Combine the sugar and corn syrup in a large, heavy saucepan over medium heat. Bring to a boil and cook at a boil until the mixture reaches the thread stage, 230°F on a candy thermometer (see page 15). Stir in the peanuts. Cook, stirring constantly, until the mixture is a light brown color and reaches the hard-crack stage, 300°F on a candy thermometer.

2. Remove from the heat, stir in the baking soda and salt, and quickly and carefully pour the mixture on a marble slab or a large sheet of parchment or waxed paper. Spread, using a rubber spatula or large-bladed knife, as thin as you can. Let cool completely, then break into pieces.

NEW YEAR'S DAY

Bloody Marys

Smothered Cabbage

Good Luck Black-Eyed Peas

New Year's Glazed Ham

Jalapeño Cornbread

Coconut Pecan Pie

"The Cajuns have many traditions and one of my favorites is about *Le Petit Bon Homme Janvier,* the little man of January. He comes every New Year's Eve, much like Santa Claus comes on Christmas Eve. When little children wake up on New Year's Day, they will find a sack or old stocking left by the little man. It usually contains oranges, pecans, and maybe a small toy, or some candy wrapped in paper. When I was little, it always had an apple, a banana, and a big peppermint stick. And we were so grateful that the apple and the banana were all ours. We didn't have to turn it over to put in a dish or return it to the kitchen. It was ours to keep. Can you imagine something so simple was thought to be so grand?"

There are times when the weather surprises us here in south Louisiana. Many times New Year's Day is warm (in the seventies) and balmy. Then again, it can be freezing cold. But no matter what the weather, many of the families gather for this special day for a traditional southern meal at their respective homes on the Island.

The tables are set with old family heirlooms, silverware, crystal, and linen. More often than not, the New Year's Day meal is served at midday, in order to allow family members and guests to enjoy a leisurely afternoon that may include a drive or a walk around the Island. The landscape may be dreary and gray, but it's always fascinating to go exploring. You may see a flock of ducks, flying in V formation, heading to the outlying marsh, or hear the whining of a boat engine in the distance—a fisherman going out to check his crab nets. Even Bird City, unpopulated at this time of year but intriguing nonetheless, is a favorite spot to linger on a brisk, cool afternoon listening to the sounds of silence.

Most of the recipes for New Year's Day are those that have been prepared for years on the Island. But that's what makes it so special—the tradition of it all.

"I like to welcome the New Year and think of it as a day to reflect not only on what has passed, but also what lies ahead," Eula Mae says.

"I like to welcome the New Year and think of it as a day to reflect not only on what has passed, but also what lies ahead."

"**N**ow tell me, what could be better than a fiery Bloody Mary made with Tabasco brand Bloody Mary mix? This drink has long been a favorite, even before the mix was bottled and sold on the market. A dash or two of Tabasco has always jazzed up Bloody Marys," says Eula Mae. "You know, Willie 'Chief' Robertson learned to make a perfect Bloody Mary for Mr. Walter. Chief is still around, and he always has the Tabasco Bloody Mary mix out on the bar whenever he comes to serve a party."

The drinks are usually served garnished with a wedge of lime. "Darling, that will certainly get everyone's juices flowing!"

BLOODY MARYS

Tabasco brand Bloody Mary mix (there are 2 kinds on the market—one mildly seasoned and one with lime juice, well seasoned)

Vodka

Add 3 to 4 parts of the mix to 1 part vodka. Serve over crushed ice and stir well. Garnish with a lime wedge or your favorite garnish, such as a celery stick or a pickled green bean.

According to local tradition, you must eat cabbage on New Year's Day if you want to be wealthy. Sometimes the cabbage is made into cole slaw, but more often than not, the favored dish is smothered cabbage.

"I add salt meat to the pot to give the dish a lot of flavor. Now, remember, some salt meat is saltier than others, but I usually boil it a bit before I add it to the pot. Just be sure to check the dish for seasoning. Sometimes the salt meat has enough salt, but sometimes you have to add it."

SMOTHERED CABBAGE

MAKES 4 TO 6 SERVINGS

$^{1}/_{4}$ cup vegetable oil

$^{3}/_{4}$ pound salt meat, trimmed, cut into 1-inch cubes, boiled in enough water to cover for 30 minutes, and drained

1 head white cabbage (about 2 pounds), cored and coarsely chopped

1 cup chopped yellow onions

1 cup water

1 tablespoon sugar

$^{1}/_{4}$ teaspoon salt

$^{1}/_{4}$ teaspoon freshly ground black pepper

$^{1}/_{4}$ teaspoon cayenne

1. Heat the oil in a large, heavy pot or Dutch oven over medium heat. Add the salt meat and cook, stirring, for 2 minutes. Add the cabbage, onions, and water, stir to mix, cover, and reduce the heat to medium-low. Cook, stirring occasionally, for 30 minutes.

2. Add the sugar, salt, black pepper, and cayenne and stir to mix. Cover and cook, stirring often, for 30 minutes longer. Serve hot.

"**E**ating black-eyed peas on New Year's Day is said to bring you good luck in the coming year, so we eat as many as we can," says Eula Mae.

"When I can, I use fresh black-eyed peas, but you can also use dried ones. No matter when I fix these peas, I can expect someone coming into the kitchen asking for a taste. The aroma is wonderful! Now, remember, this has to cook long and slow. You want the final result to be creamy and seasoned just right."

GOOD LUCK BLACK-EYED PEAS

MAKES 6 SERVINGS

1 pound fresh or dried black-eyed peas, rinsed and picked over

1 cup chopped yellow onions

2 garlic cloves, peeled

1 quart water, or more as needed

¾ teaspoon salt

½ teaspoon freshly ground black pepper

¼ teaspoon Tabasco brand pepper sauce

½ pound smoked sausage or smoked ham, chopped

¼ cup chopped fresh parsley leaves

½ cup chopped green onions (green and white parts)

Hot cooked long-grain white rice (see page 171)

1. Combine the peas, onions, garlic, water, salt, black pepper, Tabasco, and sausage in a large, heavy pot or Dutch oven. Bring to a boil, then reduce the heat to medium-low and simmer until the peas are tender and creamy, 45 minutes for fresh peas and about 2 hours for dried.

2. Stir in the parsley and green onions and cook for about 2 minutes longer.

3. Serve either over hot cooked rice or mixed together with it.

A baked ham goes a long way at gatherings on New Year's Day. It can be offered with assorted sandwich rolls and condiments such as mayonnaise and Creole mustard (or another whole-grain mustard). The bone from the ham can always be used later to flavor split pea or white bean soup.

NEW YEAR'S GLAZED HAM

MAKES ABOUT 12 SERVINGS

1 picnic ham (about 10 pounds)

¼ cup honey

¼ cup firmly packed light brown sugar

1 teaspoon dry mustard

One 15-ounce can pineapple rings, drained and juice reserved

Maraschino cherries

Whole cloves

1. Rinse the ham under cool tap water, then put in a deep, heavy pot or Dutch oven. Add enough water to cover the ham, bring to a boil, and let boil, uncovered, over medium-high heat for 1 hour. Skim away any foam that rises to the surface. Remove the ham from the pot and let cool. When cool enough to handle, remove the skin and excess fat.

2. Preheat the oven to 350°F. Put the ham in a large roasting pan and bake for 1 hour.

3. Meanwhile, combine the honey, brown sugar, mustard, and ¼ cup of the reserved pineapple juice in a small saucepan over medium heat. Whisk until the sugar dissolves and the mixture is smooth. Remove from the heat.

4. Remove the ham from the oven and brush the glaze mixture over the ham. Reduce the oven temperature to 250°F and bake for another hour.

5. Remove from the oven and arrange the pineapple slices with a cherry in the center of each (securing with toothpicks) and dot the top of the ham with the cloves. Return the ham to the oven and bake for another 20 minutes.

6. Remove from the oven and let sit for about 10 minutes before slicing to serve.

"When I have an *envie*—a desire—for something good to eat, I often make this cornbread. It doesn't have to be for a special occasion. This is one of those things that people just love to eat on its own, or to accompany any meal, like this one. You can add more or less jalapeño peppers. Always make it to your taste. But, darling, don't make it too hot, you won't enjoy the rest of the meal."

JALAPEÑO CORNBREAD

MAKES 20 PIECES

$1^1/_2$ cups finely chopped yellow onions

$^1/_4$ cup seeded and chopped red bell peppers

$^1/_2$ cup vegetable oil

1 cup yellow or white cornmeal

$^1/_2$ teaspoon salt

$^1/_2$ teaspoon baking soda

2 large eggs, well beaten

1 cup milk

$^1/_4$ cup chopped Tabasco brand pickled jalapeño peppers, or to taste

1 cup canned cream-style corn

$^1/_2$ pound mild Cheddar cheese, grated

1. Preheat the oven to 350°F. Lightly oil an 8 x 11-inch baking pan. Put it in the oven to heat for 2 to 3 minutes.

2. Meanwhile, in a large mixing bowl, combine all the ingredients and mix well. Pour into the prepared pan. Bake until it sets and is lightly golden on top, 45 minutes to 1 hour.

3. Remove from the oven and let sit for 3 to 4 minutes to cool before cutting into 2-inch squares to serve.

South Louisianians love a cup of strong, dark coffee at just about any time of day. And because the coffee is so powerful, they usually take it in a *demitasse*, a small cup. Sweetened with just a pinch of sugar and a couple of drops of cream to smooth out the flavor, the coffee goes well with just about any dessert.

The day we made this pie, Eula Mae served me a slice and complemented it with a cup of that good coffee. Perfection!

"A lot of men have a sweet tooth, but some of the ladies also like something sweet at the end of a meal, so I usually include this pie at luncheons. In fact, I make two or three because someone always wants to take a slice home!"

COCONUT PECAN PIE

MAKES ONE 9-INCH PIE; SERVES 6

1½ cups sugar
3 large eggs, beaten
½ cup (1 stick) butter, at room temperature
2 teaspoons fresh lemon juice
1 teaspoon pure vanilla extract
One 8-ounce can sweetened flaked coconut
½ cup pecan pieces
1 Basic Pie Crust (page 136)

1. Preheat the oven to 350°F.

2. In a large mixing bowl, combine the sugar, eggs, butter, lemon juice, vanilla, coconut, and pecans. Pour the mixture into the pie crust and bake until lightly golden on top, about 30 minutes.

3. Let cool before slicing to serve.

THE TRAPPER'S CAMP

Fried Catfish Fingers

Papa's Old-Time Crawfish Omelette

Fancy Crawfish Omelette

Country Crawfish Étouffée

Seafood Boil

Sara's Good Stuff

The late Walter S. McIlhenny built the trapper's camp in the 1960s. When it was erected, Mr. Walter allowed, and indeed encouraged, some of the men who worked for the McIlhennys to use it.

Raleigh Rogers and Raymond Bonin, who work for the company at "the shop" (the company mechanical shop), remember the old days.

"The building is about forty feet square with four rooms. Each trapper had a room. We stayed there sometimes three months at a time during the trapping season, which was usually December through February." They trapped the nutria, mink, muskrats, raccoons, and otters that thrive in the marsh.

Interestingly, there has been much controversy regarding nutria in recent years. A nutria resembles a small beaver, with a ratlike tail. It has large orange-red incisor teeth and partially webbed hind feet. It has caused serious erosion and damaged much of the marshland in southern Louisiana. For years, E. A. McIlhenny, who raised nutria on the Island, has been blamed for releasing them into the wild. But new information has come to light, thanks to Shane K. Bernard, McIlhenny Company historian and curator.

"E. A. did indeed, purposely, release nutria into the wild in the 1940s. However, and most significantly, it nonetheless remains true that he was not the first or even the second nutria farmer in Louisiana, and he was not the first to set loose his nutria into the state's wild on purpose. He never imported his nutria from Argentina, as was first believed, but rather he purchased them from a pre-existing nutria farm in St. Bernard Parish. In short, E. A. was partly responsible for introducing nutria to the wild, but he was not entirely so."

The marsh of south Louisiana is a blending of land and earth, water and silt, and deceptively appears to be nothing more than an expanse of swaying grasses blowing in the wind. But the five million or so acres of marshland bordering Louisiana's coast, extending inland from ten to sixty miles, sustains a year-round concentration of plant and animal life. The marshes, with the bright sunshine, thick black soil, and protected brackish waters, provide an extensive nursery and haven for fish, crustaceans, and water birds.

To get to the trapper's camp, one must travel by boat on Petite Anse Bayou, which flows through the Island, then on the Intracoastal Canal, then into a smaller unmarked waterway. The structure itself is built on stilts eight to nine feet above the marsh. The drying shelter and stretching racks for the pelts are still preserved on the property. Very traditional and rustic, it is built with old, wide cypress boards, which can withstand the damp and humid weather.

"We used to get about sixty dollars per pelt, now we get only about a dollar," explains Rogers. "We don't trap much anymore."

But the structure has continued to be maintained. The McIlhennys often take travel and food writers, who visit the Island, to see how a trapper's life used to be, and to entertain them with a meal.

"We go often in the spring because it's so lush and beautiful then. There's still a wood-burning stove that is useable, and sometimes we take the food on the boat with us when we go, and enjoy lunch overlooking the lush landscape. There's nothing like eating a meal outdoors—the food always tastes better, especially in the spring when the weather is ideal!" says Eula Mae.

"**O**ur reason for going to the camp, any camp for that matter, is to cook and eat. We think nothing of toting a black cast-iron skillet along and bringing the fresh catfish in an ice chest. I pack oil and all the ingredients in storage containers and, before you know it, we're ready to cook!"

People not from south Louisiana are sometimes apprehensive about eating catfish because they are bottom feeders. But the catfish from the bayous and waterways in south Louisiana are sweet and tasty, so much so that there is a festival (the Louisiana Catfish Festival in Des Allemands held every July) honoring the highly regarded fish.

The catfish are often cut into pieces the size of a finger, thus the name "catfish fingers." The secret, according to Eula Mae, to preparing perfectly fried catfish is in the seasoning and having the oil heated to the right temperature, about 360°F.

"These catfish fingers are crunchy on the outside, and oh, so moist on the inside! You're going to like these, I know. Remember to fry the catfish right before you serve because you want them piping hot," says Eula Mae.

Serve with Cocktail Sauce (page 192) or Tartar Sauce (page 193).

FRIED CATFISH FINGERS

MAKES 6 TO 8 APPETIZER SERVINGS

4 catfish fillets (about 7 ounces each)
$^1/_4$ cup Tabasco brand garlic pepper sauce
$^1/_2$ teaspoon salt
$^1/_2$ teaspoon Accent seasoning
$^1/_4$ teaspoon freshly ground black pepper
4 cups vegetable oil for deep-frying
2 cups Zatarain's Wonderful Fish-Fri (see Source Guide, page 223)

1. Cut the fillets into strips, each about 3 inches by 1 inch. Put in a shallow bowl with the Tabasco and stir to coat evenly. Let sit for about 20 minutes. Drain.

2. Season the fish with the salt, Accent, and black pepper. Toss to mix.

3. Meanwhile, heat the vegetable oil in a large, deep pot or electric fryer to 360°F.

4. Put the Fish-Fri in a large brown paper bag. Add the fish to the paper bag and shake the bag to coat the fish evenly. Add 8 to 10 pieces at a time to the hot oil and fry until golden brown, about 5 minutes. Drain on paper towels or on brown paper bags and serve immediately.

Cocktail sauce, in which boiled or fried seafood is dipped, is quite popular. Recipes can change from house to house, restaurant to restaurant. There is no wrong or right way to make it, as long as it satisfies the taste buds.

Eula Mae's philosophy is simple: "Taste as you make the sauce. Add a little more of this, or less of that, but, of course, never leave out the Tabasco sauce!" Make it a day ahead of time to let the flavors blend.

Cocktail Sauce

MAKES ABOUT 2 1/2 CUPS

1/4 cup finely chopped green onions (green and white parts)

2 tablespoons seeded and finely chopped red bell pepper

2 tablespoons seeded and finely chopped green bell pepper

2 tablespoons seeded and finely chopped yellow bell pepper

1 cup mayonnaise

1/2 cup prepared chili sauce

1/2 cup ketchup

1 garlic clove, pressed

Salt, freshly ground black pepper, and Tabasco brand pepper sauce to taste

1. Combine all of the ingredients and stir to mix well.

2. Cover and refrigerate for at least 1 hour before using. The sauce will keep in an airtight container in the refrigerator for up to 3 days.

Because lots of seafood is consumed in south Louisiana, remoulade sauce, cocktail sauce, and this tartar sauce are quite popular. Tartar sauce, tart and lemony, can be used to dab on fried fish, fried shrimp, or any seafood for that matter, as well as fried vegetables. Make it a day or so in advance so that the flavors come together.

"Keep it chilled until you're ready to serve. You'll see how good the cold sauce is on warm or room temperature seafood," advises Eula Mae.

Tartar Sauce

MAKES ABOUT 2^1/$_2$ CUPS

3 tablespoons finely chopped sweet pickles

1 tablespoon finely chopped dill pickles

^{1}/$_4$ cup finely chopped red onions

2 tablespoons finely chopped green onions (green and white parts)

1 tablespoon seeded and finely chopped red bell pepper

2 garlic cloves, pressed

2 teaspoons fresh lemon juice

1 teaspoon white pepper

1 teaspoon Tabasco brand pepper sauce

2 cups mayonnaise

1 tablespoon chopped fresh parsley leaves

1. Combine all the ingredients, except the parsley, in a medium-size mixing bowl. Mix well, then fold in the parsley.

2. Cover and chill for at least 1 hour before serving. The sauce will keep in an airtight container in the refrigerator for up to 3 days.

Crawfish Omelettes

You can call them what you like—crawfish, crayfish, crawdads, or mudbugs—these freshwater crustaceans are not only tasty, but versatile. Clever cooks of south Louisiana have boiled them, simmered them in stews, and stuffed the heads to use in a grand bisque (page 32) the likes of which you'll not find anywhere. They have fried them, tossed them in salads and with pasta, and put them in numerous sauces and stuffings or in omelettes like this.

"*Chère*, omelettes are not just for breakfast. These can be served anytime, and what better time than at the camp. All you need is a good skillet, some crawfish, and a few other ingredients that are easily packed in an ice chest to bring along."

Before the late 1950s, crawfish were caught in swampy waters by fishermen who used them primarily for consumption by their own families. They were rarely served in restaurants because the locals didn't want visitors watching them "peeling, squeezing, and sucking" the delectable crawfish.

But all that changed when clever businessmen and women of Breaux Bridge (a quaint town about twenty-five miles north of Avery Island) persuaded the Louisiana legislature in 1958 to declare the town "*la Capitale Mondiale de l'Écrevisse*" (the crawfish capital of the world). In 1959, Breaux Bridge celebrated its centennial with a splendid festival so well received that in 1960 the first Crawfish Festival was held with great success. The festival is celebrated every year on the first weekend of May.

Now crawfish is a booming industry in south Louisiana. There are crawfish farmers and operations that peel and boil crawfish for fresh or frozen tails that are shipped all over the country and abroad.

Eula Mae remembers that when she was growing up, the appearance of the food was not that important. More often than not, food was either served directly from the pot, or in side dishes from the kitchen or sideboard.

"But these days, everything that comes from the home kitchen or the professional kitchen must also look good. I'll show you two ways to make these omelettes— remember each will taste about the same, but one will look better. *Attendre!* Wait and see! Oh, and get fresh, not frozen, crawfish tails if you can," says Eula Mae.

Here is the mixture used in the omelette.

CRAWFISH MIXTURE

1/4 cup (1/2 stick) butter

1 cup finely chopped yellow onions

1/4 cup finely chopped celery

1/4 cup seeded and finely chopped green bell peppers

1 pound peeled crawfish tails

1/4 teaspoon salt

Pinch of freshly ground black pepper

1/8 teaspoon Tabasco brand pepper sauce

Melt the butter in a large, heavy skillet over medium heat. Add the onions and cook, stirring, until lightly golden, about 5 minutes. Add the celery and bell peppers, reduce the heat to medium-low, and cook, stirring occasionally until just soft, about 2 minutes. Add the crawfish tails, salt, black pepper, and Tabasco and cook, stirring, until a little liquid is thrown off by the crawfish, 3 to 4 minutes. Remove from the heat and divide the mixture equally between two bowls. Set aside.

PAPA'S OLD-TIME CRAWFISH OMELETTE

Half of the crawfish mixture (see page 195) mixed with $1/2$ cup chopped white button
   mushrooms

5 large eggs beaten with 3 tablespoons cool water

$1/2$ teaspoon salt

$1/8$ teaspoon Tabasco brand pepper sauce

$3/4$ cup finely chopped green onions (green and white parts)

$1/2$ cup grated Cheddar cheese for garnish (optional)

1. Spread the crawfish mixture evenly over the bottom of a 9-inch heavy skillet set over medium heat and cook for 1 minute.

2. Meanwhile, combine the egg-water mixture, salt, Tabasco, and green onions in a medium-size mixing bowl. Pour the egg mixture over the crawfish mixture and gently tip the pan to make sure the eggs are distributed evenly in the pan. With a small, narrow metal spatula or thin knife, loosen the edges, allowing the egg mixture to spread to the outer edges. Cook until the mixture sets, 5 to 6 minutes.

3. Bring the pan to the table, cut into wedges, and serve hot. Sprinkle with the cheese if you wish. (This is so much easier to serve than the following omelette when you have a large crowd.)

FANCY CRAWFISH OMELETTE

MAKES 2 SERVINGS

2 tablespoons butter

$1/2$ cup sliced white button mushrooms

Half of the crawfish mixture (see page 195)

4 large eggs beaten with 2 tablespoons cool water

$1/4$ teaspoon salt

Pinch of freshly ground black pepper

$1/8$ teaspoon Tabasco brand pepper sauce

1 tablespoon finely chopped green onions (green and white parts) for garnish

$1/2$ cup grated Cheddar cheese for garnish (optional)

1. Melt the butter in a large, heavy skillet over medium heat. Add the mushrooms and cook until just soft, about 1 minute. With a slotted spoon, transfer the mushrooms to the crawfish mixture.

2. Combine the egg mixture with the salt, black pepper, and Tabasco. Pour the mixture into the skillet and swirl over medium heat until it just begins to set. Arrange the crawfish mixture over half the eggs and gently fold the other half over it. Gently press together with a spatula and cook for about 1 minute.

3. Transfer to a serving plate and garnish with the green onions and cheese, if you wish. Serve warm.

When crawfish are in season, roughly from January to June, the locals love to entertain guests by serving several crawfish dishes at one meal. It's like having your very own festival!

Crawfish étouffée is probably the quintessential dish of south Louisiana, perhaps even more so than jambalaya and gumbo. The word *étouffer* simply means "to smother." In cooking it has another meaning, which is "to smother in its own juices." Onions, bell peppers, and celery, the vegetables often referred to as "the Trinity," which are used in many south Louisiana traditional dishes, are cooked in butter, then the crawfish are added and cooked for a short time. During this cooking the crawfish "throw off" their juices, making a wonderful gravy. Purists will tell you that no roux is used in making a traditional *étouffée*. If a roux is added, then you have a stew or a gumbo.

Most of the crawfish that's marketed for local consumption, as well as those shipped to other retail outlets, are raised in ponds. The ponds also double as rice fields later in the year. For years, crawfish fat, packed in small bags, was sold along with the crawfish, but because of its short shelf life, that is no more.

Eula Mae offers this tip: "Do not overcook the crawfish or they will become tough. The peeled crawfish tails are very delicate, so treat them as such!"

COUNTRY CRAWFISH ÉTOUFFÉE

MAKES 4 SERVINGS

$^1/_2$ cup (1 stick) butter

$1^1/_2$ cups chopped yellow onions

$^1/_2$ cup chopped celery

$^3/_4$ cup seeded and chopped green bell peppers

2 tablespoons all-purpose flour

1 cup water

1 pound peeled crawfish tails

$^3/_4$ teaspoon salt

$^1/_4$ teaspoon Tabasco brand pepper sauce

2 tablespoons chopped green onions (green and white parts)

2 tablespoons finely chopped fresh parsley leaves

4 cups hot cooked long-grain white rice (see page 171)

1. Melt the butter in a medium-size saucepan over medium heat. Add the onions and cook, stirring occasionally, until soft and lightly golden, 8 to 10 minutes. Add the celery and bell peppers and cook, stirring occasionally, until soft, about 5 minutes. Cook until the butter separates, then sprinkle with the flour and stir to blend until the mixture thickens slightly. Add the water and reduce the heat to low. Stir to blend.

2. Season the crawfish with the salt and Tabasco and add to the pot. Add the green onions and parsley and cook for about 10 minutes. Remove from the heat and serve over the rice.

Until you've experienced a seafood boil in south Louisiana, you won't understand why it's so popular. Crawfish, either from ponds or the waters of nearby Atchafalaya Basin; crabs, known as blue crabs in south Louisiana and trapped in the inshore brackish waters in bays just off the Island; and shrimp from the bays and the Gulf of Mexico are prepared in separate large pots set over butane burners. Just about everyone worth his salt has a "rig" (the large pots and butane burners) for these occasions. More often than not, a family gathering may include as many as twenty-five to fifty guests. Preparing boiled seafood for this many people wouldn't be easy in a home kitchen, so the rigs are set up outside, ideally in the shade of the majestic live oaks that thrive on the Island.

At boils on the Island, some of the pepper mash from the factory where Tabasco sauce is made is added to the pots to give the seafood a *bon goût* (a good taste). Most of the time corn on the cob, whole potatoes, and whole onions are also added to the pots, where they absorb the seasonings, giving them an amazing flavor.

Once the seafood is cooked, everything is spread out on newspaper-covered tables under the trees. Everyone stands or sits, elbow to elbow, around the tables and peels, eats, drinks, and talks for the better part of the day.

"We certainly know how to pass a good time here in south Louisiana," remarks Eula Mae.

Just about every cook around here has a different recipe for boiling seafood. This is just a guide to get you started. You can experiment with the seasonings. Some may prefer more pepper and less salt, or you may want to add cloves of fresh garlic to the pot. Experimenting is half the fun!

SEAFOOD BOIL

FOR BOILED CRAWFISH
(in Louisiana, about 5 pounds of boiled crawfish is the usual serving for 1 person)

6 gallons water

3 large yellow onions, quartered

6 to 8 medium-size red potatoes

3 large lemons, cut in half

6 fresh ears of corn, husked and silk removed (frozen corn on the cob can also be used)

1¼ cups salt

¾ cup cayenne

¼ cup Tabasco brand pepper sauce (optional)

15 pounds live crawfish, washed in cool water

1. Bring the water to a boil in a large 10-gallon pot. Add the onions, potatoes, lemons, corn, salt, cayenne, and Tabasco, if using. Cover the pot and cook until the onions and potatoes are just tender, about 20 minutes.

2. Add the crawfish, cover the pot, and bring to a boil again. Cook for 5 to 7 minutes. Drain and serve the crawfish hot with the onions, potatoes, and corn.

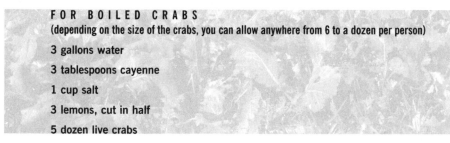

FOR BOILED CRABS
(depending on the size of the crabs, you can allow anywhere from 6 to a dozen per person)

3 gallons water

3 tablespoons cayenne

1 cup salt

3 lemons, cut in half

5 dozen live crabs

1. Combine the water, cayenne, salt, and lemons in a large pot and bring to a boil.

2. Add the crabs, cover, and bring back to a boil. When steam appears from the edge of the lid, cook 10 minutes longer, leaving the lid on. Drain and serve hot.

FOR BOILED SHRIMP
(allow about ¾ pound per serving)

1 gallon water

1 large lemon, thinly sliced

1 large yellow onion, quartered

¼ cup cayenne

1 cup salt

3 pounds shrimp, heads and shells on

1. Combine the water, lemon, onion, cayenne, and salt in a large, heavy pot. Bring to a boil and simmer for 10 minutes.

2. Add the shrimp, bring back to a boil, and cook for 3 to 5 minutes. Drain and serve hot.

"One day I was cooking for some guests on the Island and decided to prepare this dessert that I've been making for years, though there was never a name for it. One of the guests had an eight-year-old daughter who liked the dessert so much she referred to it as 'that good stuff,' so I gave it the name of Sara's Good Stuff."

SARA'S GOOD STUFF

MAKES 12 TO 14 SERVINGS

1 cup coarsely ground pecans

1 cup all-purpose flour

$^1/_2$ cup (1 stick) butter, melted

One 8-ounce package cream cheese, at room temperature

1 cup confectioners' sugar

1 teaspoon clear vanilla flavoring

One 3-ounce box chocolate instant pudding

2 cups half-and-half

One 3-ounce box vanilla instant pudding

3 cups heavy cream, beaten to soft peaks

$^1/_4$ cup chopped pecans, lightly toasted (see Note on page 140)

Chocolate curls or grated chocolate (optional)

1. Preheat the oven to 350°F.

2. Combine the pecans and flour in a medium-size mixing bowl. Add the melted butter and stir with a fork until well blended. Pat this mixture over the bottom of a 12 x 8-inch glass dish and bake until it sets, about 20 minutes. Remove from the oven and let cool completely.

3. In a large mixing bowl, beat the cream cheese, confectioners' sugar, and vanilla until fluffy. Spread the mixture evenly over the pecan crust.

4. Make the chocolate pudding with 1 cup of the half-and-half. Make the vanilla pudding with the remaining 1 cup half-and-half.

5. Gently fold one third of the heavy cream into the chocolate pudding and one third into the vanilla pudding. Spread the chocolate mixture over the cream cheese mixture, then spread the vanilla mixture over the chocolate layer. Spread the remaining heavy cream over the top. Sprinkle with the pecans. Garnish with the chocolate curls or grated chocolate if you like.

6. Cover and refrigerate for at least for at least 6 hours before serving in dessert bowls.

ISLAND MARDI GRAS

Short Rib Jambalaya

Grillades

Baked Cheese Grits

Spoon Bread

Eula Mae's Cloud Biscuits

Mini Doughnuts

The Carnival season opens on Twelfth Night (the twelfth day after Christmas), also known as the Feast of the Epiphany, which officially ends the Christmas season. Carnival is the season of merriment that begins on January 6 and ends at midnight on Mardi Gras, known as Shrove Tuesday.

During the season, which can last for several weeks, there are many parties all over Louisiana. In New Orleans, there are numerous parades and balls, luncheons and brunches, after-parade parties and before-parade parties. But on Avery Island, the festivities are more restrained.

"Oh, there are parades and balls in nearby Lafayette and New Iberia, but things are, for the most part, quiet on the Island," Eula Mae explained to me.

Years ago, in the rural areas of south Louisiana, children would don makeshift costumes—capes made with flour sacking, masks made of cardboard and tied with string, and hats of all kinds decorated with feathers or ribbons—and run along the sidewalks in the small towns. But sadly, that is no more. Today, families and guests may gather on the Island for a festive brunch or leisurely meal that lasts all day.

It's best to have lots of food around on Mardi Gras. Guests come and go throughout the day. And some might have a "heavy" head from too much partying the night before and need some good food to help them along. The menu on Mardi Gras runs the gamut from jambalaya to grillades and grits. "The main thing," Eula Mae says, "is that everyone gets together to visit and enjoy a good meal.

In New Orleans, there are numerous parades and balls, luncheons and brunches, after-parade parties and before-parade parties.

Jambalaya can be made with just about anything—chicken, sausage, seafood, rabbit, ducks—that is at hand. Eula Mae claims that this short-rib jambalaya is one of the best because of the flavor from the pork ribs. She explained her secret to making this one.

"To make a good jambalaya, you need to get the *grimilles*—browned bits—in the bottom of the pot to give the dish that wonderful golden brown color. While cooking the onions and meat, scrape the bottom and sides of the pot often with a spoon or spatula."

SHORT RIB JAMBALAYA

MAKES 8 TO 10 SERVINGS

1 tablespoon vegetable oil

2 pounds pork short ribs, cut into 2-inch pieces

3 teaspoons salt

$1/2$ teaspoon freshly ground black pepper

$1/2$ teaspoon Accent seasoning

2 teaspoons Tabasco brand pepper sauce

$1^1/2$ cups chopped yellow onions

$1/2$ cup chopped celery

3 garlic cloves, peeled

1 cup seeded and chopped bell peppers (green, red, and yellow mixed or just green)

$3/4$ cup canned seeded and chopped tomatoes

4 cups water

$1/3$ cup chopped fresh parsley leaves

$1/2$ cup finely chopped green onions (green and white parts)

3 cups raw long-grain white rice

1. Oil a large, heavy pot or Dutch oven with the vegetable oil and place over medium heat. Season the ribs with 2 teaspoons of the salt, $1/4$ teaspoon of the black pepper, the Accent, and 1 teaspoon of the Tabasco. When the oil is hot, add the ribs and cover the pot. Cook, stirring occasionally and scraping the browned bits from the bottom of the pan, until the meat is evenly browned, about 45 minutes.

2. Transfer the ribs to a platter and drain off all but 3 tablespoons of the fat in the pot. Add the onions and cook, stirring occasionally and scraping the browned bits off the bottom of the pot, until they are soft and lightly golden, 5 to 6 minutes. Add the celery and garlic and cook for 5 minutes, stirring occasionally. Add the bell peppers and cook, stirring a few times, for 2 to 3 minutes. Add the tomatoes and return the ribs to the pot. Cover and cook over medium-low heat for 30 minutes, stirring occasionally.

3. Add the water, cover, and simmer for 30 minutes longer. Add the parsley, green onions, and rice. With a spoon, stir to submerge the rice in the liquid. Add the remaining 1 teaspoon salt, $\frac{1}{4}$ teaspoon black pepper, and 1 teaspoon Tabasco. Stir to mix, cover, and cook until all the liquid is absorbed, about 30 minutes.

4. Remove from the heat and let stand, covered, for about 5 minutes before serving.

Grillades (pronounced gree-yawds) has been served for breakfast, lunch, and brunch on the Island for years. It is a dish that combines all the basic ingredients found in the cuisine of south Louisiana. Onions, bell peppers, and garlic are cooked until golden and soft, then tomatoes are added and simmered with small pieces of beef or veal. The result is delicious and filling.

"As far as I'm concerned, this dish is a must for parties on the Island. It has to cook long and slow for the best results, and I always cook it a day ahead so that the flavors can come together. And don't forget to serve them with grits," says Eula Mae.

GRILLADES

4 pounds veal rounds, about $1/2$ inch thick

$1/2$ cup bacon drippings

$1/2$ cup all-purpose flour

$1^1/2$ cups seeded and chopped green bell peppers

1 cup chopped yellow onions

3 garlic cloves, minced

2 cups canned plum tomatoes, chopped, with their liquid

$3/4$ teaspoon dried thyme

$1^1/2$ cups beef broth

1 cup dry red wine

2 tablespoons Worcestershire sauce

1 tablespoon Tabasco brand pepper sauce

1 tablespoon salt

$1/2$ teaspoon freshly ground black pepper

2 bay leaves

3 tablespoons finely chopped fresh parsley leaves

1 recipe Baked Cheese Grits (page 210)

1. Trim any fat from the veal and cut into 2-inch squares. With a meat mallet, pound each piece to $1/4$-inch thickness.

2. Heat ¼ cup of the bacon drippings in a large, heavy pot or Dutch oven over medium-high heat. Add the veal, in batches, and brown evenly on both sides. Transfer to a warm platter as they are cooked.

3. Reduce the heat to medium and add the remaining ¼ cup bacon drippings and the flour to the pot. Cooking slowly and constantly, make a dark brown roux (see Eula Mae's advice for making a roux, page 94). Add the bell peppers, onions, and garlic and cook, stirring often, until soft, about 5 minutes. Add the tomatoes and thyme and cook, stirring occasionally, for 3 minutes. Add the beef broth and wine and cook, stirring, for about 5 minutes. Return the veal to the pot and add the Worcestershire, Tabasco, salt, pepper, and bay leaves. Reduce the heat to medium-low and simmer, covered, until the veal is very tender, about 1½ hours.

4. Remove and discard the bay leaves. Stir in the parsley. Remove from the heat and let cool completely. Cover and refrigerate for 12 hours.

5. When ready to serve, reheat and serve over the cheese grits.

"People who haven't had these cheese grits are missing out on a real treat." Traditionally they are served with Grillades (page 208), but you can serve them with just about anything, like scrambled eggs and bacon, or any breakfast-brunch items.

BAKED CHEESE GRITS

MAKES 6 SERVINGS

5 cups water

1 cup yellow or white quick (regular) grits

2 cups freshly grated Cheddar cheese

$1/4$ cup ($1/2$ stick) butter

2 large eggs, lightly beaten

$1/2$ teaspoon salt

$1/4$ teaspoon garlic powder

$1/4$ teaspoon Tabasco brand pepper sauce

1. Preheat the oven to 350°F. Grease a $1\frac{1}{2}$-quart casserole or baking dish and set aside.

2. Bring the water to a boil in a large, heavy saucepan. Stir in the grits and return to a boil. Cover and simmer over low heat until thickened, 15 to 20 minutes.

3. Add the cheese and butter to the cooked grits and stir until both melt completely. Stir in the eggs, salt, garlic powder, and Tabasco and blend well. Pour the mixture into the prepared casserole and bake until it sets, 35 to 40 minutes. Remove from the oven and let stand about 5 minutes before serving.

Spoon bread is another variation of cornbread. It is more like a pudding and is often eaten with a spoon—thus the name. It's a great accompaniment to egg dishes or Grillades (page 208).

According to Eula Mae, she has a hard time finding stone-ground cornmeal.

"So, I buy one pound of regular yellow cornmeal and sift it. I use the first sifting to coat fish to fry, then use the coarse meal that's left after the sifting for this spoon bread."

SPOON BREAD

MAKES ABOUT 6 SERVINGS

$^3/_4$ cup water

1 teaspoon salt

$^1/_4$ cup white quick-cooking (regular) grits

$^1/_4$ cup ($^1/_2$ stick) butter

1 cup milk

3 large eggs, separated

$1^1/_2$ cups coarse-ground yellow cornmeal

2 teaspoons baking powder

1. Preheat the oven to 350°F. Butter an 8-inch square baking dish. Set aside.

2. Bring the water to a boil in the top of a double boiler. Add the salt and grits and stir for about 2 minutes. Place over the bottom of the boiler, filled with simmering water, and cook, stirring occasionally, until the mixture thickens, about 20 minutes. Add the butter, milk, egg yolks, and the cornmeal sifted with the baking powder and stir well to combine.

3. In a small mixing bowl, whisk the egg whites just until slightly foamy and stir into the cornmeal mixture.

4. Pour the mixture into the prepared dish and bake until the top is golden, about 1 hour. Remove from the oven and spoon onto serving plates.

I n the November 1992 issue of *Gourmet* magazine, Marion Cunningham featured Eula Mae's biscuits. "I've been making these biscuits since I was a child. I think I can make them in my sleep! Make several batches if you have to serve a crowd and remember, the more you sift, darling, the better—I sift four times," advises Eula Mae. "Also, it's best to have your flour, vegetable shortening, and, of course, the buttermilk well chilled before you begin. That's another of my little secrets. Because it's so hot and damp in south Louisiana, I came up with that solution to make my biscuits light as a cloud."

EULA MAE'S CLOUD BISCUITS

MAKES 12 TO 14

2 cups all-purpose flour

2 teaspoons baking powder

$^{1}/_{2}$ teaspoon baking soda

$^{1}/_{2}$ teaspoon salt

1 teaspoon sugar

$^{1}/_{3}$ cup butter-flavored Crisco vegetable shortening, chilled and cut into bits

1 cup buttermilk

2 tablespoons butter, melted

1. Preheat the oven to 450°F.

2. Sift the flour, baking powder, baking soda, salt, and sugar 4 times into a large mixing bowl.

3. Blend in the shortening with your fingertips until the mixture resembles coarse meal. Make a well in the center of the mixture and pour in the buttermilk. Using a fork and beginning in the center, stir until the buttermilk is mixed into the flour. Then mix until the dough forms a sticky ball.

4. With floured hands, transfer the dough to a well-floured work surface and knead it lightly about 8 times, but do not overwork the dough. Pat out the dough to a $^{1}/_{2}$-inch thickness. Cut out the biscuits with a floured 2-inch round cutter.

5. Line a baking sheet with parchment paper. Arrange the biscuits on the sheet, making sure they just touch each other. Pick up the trimmings, knead together, and cut more biscuits if possible. Bake until golden, 10 to 12 minutes.

6. When ready to serve, lightly brush the tops with the hot melted butter.

"**M**y daughter, Susan, loves these. I made them often for her when she was a child, but now she has a child of her own and makes the doughnuts for him. But I can tell you, adults go crazy for these. Whenever I'm cooking for a crowd, I make several batches and make sure to have lots of *café au lait* to go with them. The secret to making this doughnut batter is to slowly incorporate the flour into the wet ingredients. Don't rush. Today you can pick up doughnuts at the bakery or make them from a boxed mix, but *chère*, nothing is better than these made from scratch."

MINI DOUGHNUTS

MAKES ABOUT 14 DOUGHNUTS

3 cups all-purpose flour

1 cup granulated sugar

2 teaspoons baking powder

$1/2$ teaspoon salt

2 large eggs, well beaten

1 tablespoon butter, melted

4 to 5 tablespoons milk

1 tablespoon pure vanilla extract

$1/8$ teaspoon ground nutmeg

3 cups vegetable or peanut oil for deep-frying

Confectioners' sugar

1. Combine the flour, sugar, baking powder, and salt in a large mixing bowl and mix well.

2. Combine the eggs, melted butter, milk, vanilla, and nutmeg in a small bowl and mix well.

3. Make a well in the center of the dry ingredients, add the egg mixture, and stir in one direction with a wooden spoon until the mixture forms a ball and all the flour is incorporated. (Hold the ball in the center with a fork and run the dough around the bowl to pick up the flour on the edges of the bowl.)

4. Turn the dough out on a lightly floured work surface and pat it into a disk about $1/2$ inch thick. Use a $2^1/2$-inch biscuit cutter (or a glass) to cut out the doughnuts. Dip your index finger in some flour and punch a hole in the center of each doughnut, then turn it around your finger

to make the hole about 1½ inches in diameter. Once you put the doughnuts in the hot oil, the holes close up a bit.

5. Heat the oil in a deep, heavy pot or an electric fryer to 360°F. The oil should be deep enough so that the doughnuts float and do not touch the bottom of the pot. Add the doughnuts, 2 to 3 at a time, turning them around in the hot oil until brown. ("Usually, the dough cracks a bit and that's how I know they're done.")

6. Drain on paper towels, sprinkle with confectioners' sugar, and serve warm.

> **CROQUIGNOLES** So as not to waste the extra dough that is left, gather up the scraps and pat them into another disk about ½ inch thick. Then, using a knife, cut it in half, then in half again, and make 2 slashes in the center of each piece. You should have about 4 pieces. Fry these in the hot oil and now you have *croquignoles*, those wonderful doughnut-like cakes that the old people made years ago. Sprinkle with confectioners' sugar before serving.

> **CHOCOLATE-GLAZED DOUGHNUTS** If you wish to glaze the doughnuts, mix together ½ cup sugar and 2 tablespoons unsweetened cocoa powder, stirring well to get rid of any lumps. Transfer to a small saucepan, add 1 cup milk, and cook, stirring, until the mixture is thick and smooth. Slip a fork or thin knife through the holes in the doughnuts, dip them in the chocolate glaze to coat, and transfer to a plate. Once they have cooled completely, they can be stored in an airtight container.

SAINT PATRICK'S DAY IN ACADIANA

Cheesy Spinach Bread

Stuffed Bell Peppers

Cabbage Rolls

Pistachio Pudding and Cookies

"When I was a youngster, we didn't celebrate Saint Patrick's Day. After all, we weren't Irish and didn't know how they celebrated."

But several years ago, Mr. Paul invited several guests to join him for lunch on Saint Patrick's Day. A raconteur and *bon vivant*, he called Eula Mae the day before and asked her to prepare a "green" meal.

"Oh, Mr. Paul loves to have a good time and a good meal!" Eula Mae says, laughing and shaking her head.

"I looked out my window for inspiration. I saw that I had some green bell peppers in the garden. They would be ideal for stuffing with a rice, beef, and pork dressing. I always try to use what I can from our gardens on the Island. When we say fresh around here, we mean it. I made it a point to pick the bell peppers just before I prepared them. And there were still a few heads of cabbage to make the cabbage rolls.

"We even had green lemonade. All I did was make a pitcher of homemade lemonade and add a couple of drops of green food coloring to the pitcher to make it festive. I served it with a wedge of lime instead of lemon. It's so simple to make it fun!"

None of Eula Mae's recipes requires exotic ingredients or difficult preparations. Take this spinach bread, for instance. The French bread comes from LeJeune's Bakery in nearby Jeanerette. The LeJeune family has been baking bread since 1884 and Eula Mae swears by their product, which is baked early each morning. She thinks nothing of driving into New Iberia, about six miles away, to get the bread at a local grocery store when she wants to make this spinach bread.

"Darling," she says, "fresh is always best."

The bread, dressed with a creamy spinach-and-cheese mixture, is great to serve as an hors d'oeuvre for Saint Patrick's Day, or for any occasion for that matter. It can also be served with the meal. Add more red bell peppers to make it festive for holiday parties. And be sure to make a lot because everybody loves this treat!

CHEESY SPINACH BREAD

MAKES ABOUT 28 SLICES; SERVES 6 TO 8

$^1/_2$ cup (1 stick) butter

2 large garlic cloves, minced (about 1 tablespoon)

2 cups chopped yellow onions

$^1/_4$ cup seeded and chopped mixed red, green, and yellow bell peppers

$^1/_2$ pound white button mushrooms, wiped clean, trimmed, and thinly sliced

One 10-ounce package frozen chopped spinach, thawed and squeezed dry

$^1/_8$ teaspoon Tabasco brand garlic pepper sauce

1 cup grated mild Cheddar cheese

1 cup grated mozzarella cheese

1 large loaf French bread, about 16 inches long, split in half lengthwise

1. Preheat the oven to 350°F.

2. Melt the butter in a large skillet over medium-low heat. Add the garlic and cook, stirring a few times, for 3 to 4 minutes. Increase the heat to medium, add the onions, and cook, stirring occasionally, until they are slightly soft and golden, about 10 minutes. Add the bell peppers and mushrooms and cook, stirring occasionally, until they are soft, about 5 minutes. Add the spinach and stir to blend. Cook, stirring occasionally, for about 10 minutes.

3. Remove from the heat, add the Tabasco and cheeses, and stir until they are just slightly melted. Let cool for about 15 minutes. Divide the mixture into two equal portions and spread evenly over the bread halves.

4. Line a baking sheet with aluminum foil. Put the bread halves, spinach side up, on the foil, and bake until the bread is toasty and the spinach has browned a bit, about 20 minutes. Let cool for about 3 minutes before cutting with an electric knife ("that's the best way, darling, sometimes new gadgets do work") before serving. Cut the bread into 1-inch-thick slices on a diagonal to make it look nice.

The stuffed bell peppers are not difficult to make, but it takes time to prepare them. One day, Eula Mae and I made some for a luncheon meeting on the Island and she noticed I was growing edgy.

"You can't rush to make these. Remember, have *patience*. Your guests will always know that you took the time to make these!" she said fervently.

STUFFED BELL PEPPERS

MAKES 12 SERVINGS

$1/3$ cup raw long-grain white rice

$1^3/8$ teaspoons salt

1 teaspoon butter

3 cups water

2 ripe Roma tomatoes

3 large green bell peppers, stems neatly cut out in a lid and seeded

$1/2$ cup vegetable oil

3 tablespoons all-purpose flour

$3/4$ pound lean ground pork

$3/4$ pound lean ground beef

3 garlic cloves, peeled

$1^1/2$ cups chopped yellow onions

$1/2$ cup chopped celery

$1/4$ cup each seeded and chopped green, red, and yellow bell peppers

1 small eggplant, peeled and cubed

$1/4$ teaspoon freshly ground black pepper

$1/4$ teaspoon cayenne

$1^1/4$ cups Eula Mae's Homemade Bread Crumbs (page 34)

$1/4$ teaspoon Tabasco brand pepper sauce

$1/4$ cup chopped green onions (green and white parts)

$1/4$ cup chopped fresh parsley leaves

$1/4$ cup freshly grated Parmesan cheese

$1/4$ teaspoon sweet paprika

2 tablespoons butter, melted

1. Combine the rice, ¼ teaspoon of the salt, and the butter in a small saucepan. Add enough water to come to the first joint of your little finger. Cover the pot and bring to a boil. When it comes to a boil and steam escapes from the lid, reduce the heat to low, and cook until the rice is tender, about 20 minutes. Remove from the heat and set aside.

2. Bring the water to a boil in a medium-size saucepan over medium heat. Add the tomatoes, boil for about 1 minute, and remove from the pot. Keep the water boiling. Let the tomatoes cool, then remove the skins and coarsely chop. Set aside.

3. Add the whole green bell peppers to the boiling water, reduce the heat to medium-low, and simmer, turning often, until slightly soft, 5 to 8 minutes. Remove from the heat and drain, reserving the cooking broth. Let the peppers cool. If the stuffed peppers are going to be the entree for a luncheon, leave them whole and stand them up on end. If the peppers will be used as a side dish or served on a buffet, cut in half or quarters before stuffing. Set aside.

4. Combine the oil and the flour in a large, heavy pot over medium heat and, stirring slowly and constantly, make a roux the color of peanut butter (see page 94 for Eula Mae's advice on how to make a roux). Add the pork and beef. Cook, stirring, until the meat browns and all the pink disappears, about 5 minutes. Add the garlic and cook, stirring occasionally, for about 5 minutes. Remove from the heat and let cool for a few minutes. Drain off any excess oil. Return to the stove over medium-low heat. Add the onions, celery, and chopped peppers and cook, stirring, until soft and golden, 5 to 8 minutes. Add the tomatoes, eggplant, and ½ cup of the reserved broth. Stir to mix, cover, and cook, stirring occasionally, until the eggplant is soft, about 20 minutes. Add the remaining 1⅛ teaspoons salt, the black pepper, and cayenne and cook 5 minutes longer. Add 1 cup of the bread crumbs, the Tabasco, cooked rice, green onions, and parsley and stir to mix. Remove from the heat and let cool for 5 minutes.

5. Preheat the oven to 350°F. Combine the remaining bread crumbs, the Parmesan, and paprika in a small mixing bowl.

6. If using the whole peppers, spoon the filling mixture into the pepper to fill completely. Pat equal parts of the bread crumb-and-cheese mixture on top of each. For the halves or quarters, spoon the dressing onto the pieces of peppers and gently pat it with your fingers into a mound. Sprinkle each pepper with an equal part of the bread crumb-and-cheese mixture and pat into the dressing.

7. Arrange the peppers in a shallow pan lined with aluminum foil. Drizzle each pepper with an equal amount of the melted butter and bake until lightly golden on top, about 25 minutes. Serve warm.

These cabbage rolls are not difficult to prepare, but they do take a little time to stuff and roll. When Eula Mae set aside a day to show me how they were made, it was a bit awkward at first—placing a bit of the stuffing on the cabbage leaf, then carefully rolling it. But, with her usual kind and patient manner, she stood beside me and unhurriedly stuffed and rolled a few leaves.

"See, darling, it's really very easy. Take your time," she said.

I did and before I knew it I stuffed and rolled almost as deftly as she.

CABBAGE ROLLS

MAKES ABOUT 28 ROLLS

$^1/_2$ pound ground pork

$^1/_2$ pound ground beef

$^1/_2$ cup seeded and chopped green bell peppers

$^1/_4$ cup chopped yellow onions

One 8-ounce can tomato sauce

2 tablespoons raw long-grain white rice

2 teaspoons salt

$^1/_2$ teaspoon Tabasco brand pepper sauce

$^1/_2$ teaspoon dried thyme

1 large head green cabbage

1. Mix together the pork, beef, bell peppers, onions, tomato sauce, rice, salt, Tabasco, and thyme in a large mixing bowl.

2. Place the cabbage in a large kettle of boiling water and let boil for 10 minutes. Remove from the water and let cool for 10 minutes. Remove the core and gently peel off the leaves.

3. Place 2 tablespoons of the meat filling in the center of each leaf, fold the sides in, and then roll up.

4. Place a wire rack in a large, deep pot or Dutch oven. Add water to the depth of the rack, about 1 inch. Place the cabbage rolls on the rack, seam side down, cover, and steam for $1^1/_2$ hours. Keep the water simmering; if it evaporates, add additional water. Serve hot.

PISTACHIO PUDDING AND COOKIES

MAKES ABOUT 8 SERVINGS

1 recipe Ti Gâteau Sec (page 108)

Two 3-ounce boxes pistachio instant pudding

2 cups half-and-half

2 cups heavy cream, beaten to soft peaks

2 to 3 drops green food coloring

1. Crumble two of the cookies in the bottom of each of 8 dessert bowls.

2. Make the pudding with the half-and-half according to the package directions. Tint the heavy cream with the food coloring. Gently fold half of the cream into the pudding. Pour equal amounts of the pudding over the crumbled cookies.

3. Refrigerate until the pudding sets, about 30 minutes. When ready to serve, spoon the remaining cream equally over the pudding servings.

SOURCE GUIDE

C. S. Steen Syrup Mill
P.O. Box 339
Abbeville, LA 70510
Tel: (800) 725-1654
Fax: (337) 893-2478
www.steensyrup.com
100% pure cane syrup, dark and light molasses

www.cajungrocer.com
A good source for a variety of Louisiana products.

TABASCO Country Store
McIlhenny Company
Avery Island, LA 70513-5002
(800) 634-9599
www.TABASCO.com

Zatarain's
82 First Street
Box 347
Gretna, LA 70053
(504) 367-2950
www.zatarain.com

INDEX